DREAM FULFILLMENT

Mariá Carmen Gear, M.D.
Ernesto César Liendo, M.D.
Lila Lee Scott, M.D.

with
Felix Reyna

Jason Aronson Inc.
Northvale, New Jersey
London

Copyright © 1988 by Jason Aronson Inc.

10 9 8 7 6 5 4 3 2 1

All rights reserved. Printed in the United States of America. No part of this book may be used or reproduced in any manner whatsoever without written permission from *Jason Aronson Inc.* except in the case of brief quotations in reviews for inclusion in a magazine, newspaper, or broadcast.

The authors gratefully acknowledge permission from:
Dow Jones and Co., Inc., and *The Wall St. Journal* to quote Martha Bayles's television review of Feb. 23, 1987, "Crash Krantz Recrudesces," and the *Daily Journal* of Caracas to quote Ellen Goodman's March 1987 article "Never Enough in Money Games."

Library of Congress Cataloging-in-Publication Data

Gear, Mariá Carmen.
    Dream fulfillment / Mariá Carmen Gear, Ernesto César Liendo, and Lila Lee Scott with Felix Reyna.
    p.   cm.
    Bibliography: p.
    Includes index.
    ISBN 0-87668-912-8
    1. Dreams. 2. Self-realization. 3. Goal (Psychology)
4. Melodrama—Psychological aspects. 5. Freud, Sigmund, 1856–1939.
I. Liendo, Ernesto César. II. Scott, Lila Lee. III. Title.
BF1078.G39 1988   88-10418
154—dc19   CIP

Manufactured in the United States of America.
Jason Aronson Inc. offers books and cassettes.
For information and catalog write to
Jason Aronson Inc.
230 Livingston Street
Northvale, N.J. 07647

My love is something valuable to me which I ought not to throw away without reflection. It imposes duties on one for whose fulfillment I must be ready to make sacrifices. . . . And how could one possibly forget . . . of all others, this technique in the art of living? . . .

Nor is it content to aim at an avoidance of unpleasure—a goal, as we might call it, of weary *resignation*; it passes this by without heed and holds fast to the original, passionate striving for a positive fulfillment of *happiness*.

. . . Maybe we are never so defenseless against suffering as when we love, never so helplessly unhappy as when we have lost our love object or its love. But this does not dispose of the technique of living based on the value of love as a means to happiness.

Sigmund Freud
Civilization and Its Discontents

Previous Publications by the Authors

1. Gear, M. C., and Liendo, E. C. *Semiologie psychanalitique* (Psychoanalytic semiotics). Paris: Edition de Minuit, 1975.
2. Gear, M. C., and Liendo, E. C. *Psicoterapia della coppia e del gruppo familiare* (Couple and family psychoanalysis). Florencia: Del Riccio, 1976.
3. Gear, M. C., and Liendo, E. C. *Psicoanalisis del paciente y de su ambiente* (Psychoanalysis of the patient and his environment). Buenos Aires: Nueva Vision, 1977.
4. Gear, M. C., and Liendo, E. C. *Action Psychanalitique* (Psychoanalytic action). Paris: Minuit, 1978.
5. Gear, M. C., and Liendo, E. C. *Informatica Psicanalitica* (Psychoanalysis and informatics). Rio de Janeiro: Imago, 1979.
6. Gear, M. C., and Liendo, E. C. *Matematica psicoanalitica* (Applying methematics to psychoanalysis). Buenos Aires: Nueva Vision, 1980.
7. Gear, M. C., and Liendo, E. C. *Epistemologia psicoanalitica* (Psychoanalytic epistemology). Buenos Aires: Nueva Vision, 1980.
8. Gear, M. C., and Liendo, E. C. Metapsychology of sadism and masochism. A bipolar semiotic model. *Psychoanalysis and Contemporary Thought* 4:207, 1981.
9. Gear, M. C., Hill, M., and Liendo, E. C. *Working through narcissism*. New York: Jason Aronson, 1981.
10. Gear, M. C., and Liendo, E. C. Psychanalyse, semiologie, et communication familiale. *L'evolution Psiquiatrique* (Psychoanalysis, semiotics, and family communication). Paris: 1982.
11. Gear, M. C., Liendo, E. C., and Scott, L. L. *Patients and agents*. New York: Jason Aronson, 1983.
12. Gear, M. C., and Liendo, E. C. *Therapie familiale psychanalitique* (Psychoanalytic family therapy). Paris: Dunod, 1984.

Contents

Preface — vii
Acknowledgments — xvii

PART I   DREAMS AND OPTIONS

1 Dreams versus Illusions and Delusions — 3
2 Choosing to Transcend Together — 11
3 Early Signs of Emotional Incompetence — 21

PART II   FALSE OPTIONS

4 Choosing to Avoid Anxiety through Melodrama — 33
5 Defensive Monothematic Inverted Speech — 41

6	The Sadomasochistic and Narcissistic Monologue	49
7	Exhibitionism, Mirrorism, and Telemelodrama	59
8	Pushers and Users of the Telemelodrama	67
9	The "Not Enough Syndrome" and Drug Addiction	77

PART III NEW OPTIONS

10	Gaining Competence to Deal with One's Incompetence	89
11	Reframing and Enriching Dreams	97
12	Uncovering the Repressed Story	121
13	Stepping out of Melodrama	135

PART IV

THE PREFERRED PERSONAL OPTION

14	Implementing a Meaningful Project	155
15	Strengths, Deficits, and Project Realization	175
16	Treatment Strategy Based on Strengths and Deficits	195
	References	217
	Index	223

Preface

THIS BOOK IS about dream fulfillment. It is about the functioning of night dreams and nightmares as anticipatory signals of performance.

This work shows the relationship of the daydream to the personal project, the night dream, the "daymare," and the nightmare. The daydream centers on the fulfillment of desire through its concrete and operational expression, the personal project. The night dream and the nightmare are symbolic indicators of the individual's competence to cope with survival and have a happy and fulfilled life through achieving the daydream. A night dream is an unconscious confirmation of a state of well-being. It reflects that the person is meeting survival needs and mastering the problems that stand in the way of happiness. A nightmare occurs when survival is threatened or when the daydream is unreachable. It is an early warning of unconscious anxiety accumulated in response to failure. A "daymare" is the conscious living out of what is most feared, that is, a chaotic state due to a threat to personal survival or the realization that one's daydream is unreachable. It is the "reality shock" when the individual becomes acutely aware of his lack of mastery, or coping skills.

Instead of taking a sleeping pill to calm the anxiety that the nightmare produces, a person would do well to heed the warning and awaken fully to an understanding of how and in what vital areas he or she is failing. By confronting the failure rather than escaping to an artificially induced calm of a drugged sleep, the person has the option to resolve the underlying incompetence. There can be a return to mastery and to the active pursuit of happiness.

A lack of capacity to cope with survival needs produces a high level of anxiety and gives a sense of panic or chaos that is reflected in a nightmare or a daymare. Obviously, there is a hierarchy of needs and desires. Survival needs must be coped with before attending to the fulfillment of desire. Daymares and nightmares must be overcome before daydreams and night dreams become a source of anticipated gratification. When the defense has been resolved, the dream returns again to personal transcendence, the achieving of a project intimately related to the individual's ideal of himself. Dreams of happiness can only be realized in an intimate relationship of sharing and caring with others.

Aspirations to improve the quality of life require that the individual be prepared to confront adversity. Setbacks are predictable in ambitious projects. The danger is that the person may decide that the goal is not worth the frustration, sacrifice, and psychological pain, or that it is just another unrealizable dream when, in fact, the objective is achievable with a consistent investment of effort. This failure to accept that there is no easy way may cause the person to prematurely give up his daydreams, showing himself to be "emotionally incompetent."

This book has a double purpose. It looks to deepen the understanding of what it means emotionally to live in both a concrete and symbolic "Manhattan." Concretely, Manhattan is the center of the superdeveloped world. Symbolically, it represents "transcendence," a "making it big," a going beyond the usual to the exceptional. This book looks at "Manhattan" from a "reframed" Freudian perspective. The "reframing" consists of looking at the assumptions of the individual and the subculture of this most powerful and modern of settings, to reinterpret what is repressed, displaced, and defended against in contemporary America. Symbolically "Manhattan" signifies achievement of a higher development. All individuals have a "Manhattan" within them. Their "Manhattan dream" has the structural detail of their own personal architecture. They may wish to "make it in Manhattan" or, with equal validity, to make their hometown a better place to live.

If we accept that mental health is the capacity to produce happiness by fulfilling personal dreams of transcendence to share with intimately related others, our framing and enriching of the Freudian model would address the therapeutic task needed to facilitate enrichment of desire and an increase in personal competence. The reframing is made possible through multidisciplinary contributions that enrich and elaborate the Freudian "assumptions." Freud's paradigm is analyzed, broadened, and enhanced. The general Freudian principles are found to be still valid, although the specific content is determined by the context of nineteenth-century Vienna.

The "Manhattan phenomenon" could be considered an impacting illustration of the emotional meaning of living in a "superdeveloped" world city. Here everything seems possible and at the same time, impossible; the aspirations that people have and their available options do not necessarily coincide. This "Manhattan phenomenon" of a transcendent promise but a difficult realization is a common experience for Americans everywhere. There are differences between conscious desire and realizable dreams and discrepancies between the real and apparent means for achievement. This is true of both the socioeconomic dreams of transcendence and the interpersonal dreams of intimacy.

The perceived insufficiency of the psychoanalytic model applied to dream fulfillment results from a lack of information on the part of professional and public alike and from a literal noncontextualized interpretation of the model. The model suffers from an unfortunate sclerotic state. The closure has made it age without being allowed to mature. It has been used without flexibility. There is a need to bring it into line with current technological and scientific contributions. The authors will have fulfilled their dream if they can serve the symbolic "Freud" himself at the service of a symbolic "Manhattan." Then they will have answered Dinitia Smith's (1986) question: "What would Freud think about New York today?"

The utilization of a Freudian focus does not imply the total acceptance of all theoretical, strategic, and technical restrictions of the model. An example would be the literal interpretation of a phalocentric reductionism by which Freud placed all motivations at the genital level of development. Many concepts will be reformulated or "reframed." The function of dreams is not viewed only as a "realization of unconscious infantile sexual desire" (Freud 1900). The dream will be linked to the realization of a socialized desire, the "ideal of the ego," and to the power—the mastery or competence—necessary for survival and fulfillment of desire. This desire may be sexual or nonsexual. It is a desire of transcendence in togetherness. The interpretation of the Freudian notion of "castration complex" (Freud 1927) as a fear of losing the penis will be reformulated as a personal conviction about power. The castrated do not have the power to fulfill desire. Therefore, the complementary concept of "penis envy" will not be interpreted as woman's envy toward the masculine but as the envy of both men and women who are not competent to fulfill desire in relation to those others who are competent. It is not a biological penis but a symbolic "phallus" that is envied. This emblem of the power (Lacan 1966) to fulfill dreams is envied by both sexes. The possession of a penis does not guarantee the fulfillment of needs and desire, whereas the possession of a "phallus" does.

In order to address the problem of how to be happy in Manhattan in contemporary America, it is necessary first to guarantee survival. The survival is then made worthwhile by producing happiness to share with others. To define "happiness," the authors propose a "happiness triangle" in a dynamic relationship of three essential elements—the self, the others, and the personal project. Accordingly, to attain happiness, the self is related to a personal project through the dream of transcendence. Self and others are related through the establishment of intimate togetherness. Transcendence is considered of equal importance to togetherness.

The authors present a model of health and illness which has its origins in a multidisciplinary reframing and broadening of the Freudian perspective. The fundamentals of health were for Freud (1910), as they are for the authors, the ability to love and to work (Gear et al. 1981). He also gave central importance to the deep infantile wish. From this is established the "Ideal of the Ego" and the dream of personal transcendence. The ability to dream the dream of self-realization and to negotiate this dream with the real world seems to be essential to mental health.

The mentally ill are defined as unable to produce happiness for self and others even in favorable circumstances. They tend, rather, to create unhappiness. This tendency seems to depend on a psychological incompetence to deal with one's own incompetence in performance; that is, an incompetence to face incompetence.

The mentally healthy are defined as able to produce happiness for themselves and others in spite of difficult and unfavorable circumstances. This seems to depend on a psychological competence to face and try to overcome incompetence. This is competence to face incompetence. There is a capacity to resolve the problems around one's own transcendence and to share the happiness that results.

The key variable is the person's capacity in respect to needs, dreams, and desires. He or she must be able to conceive, recognize, and, above all, implement the fulfillment of cherished personal dreams and those of intimate others.

When the person is convinced—often with an "illusional or delusional certainty"—that it is not possible to realize his dreams, he abandons efforts to reach them. The healthy desire for sharing and for self-realization is "perverted" (Aulagnier 1966). The person feels compelled to escape from anxiety. He succumbs to an unconscious interpersonal compulsion and repeats a stereotyped interpersonal defensive behavior of mistreatment that is perceived in reverse. The mistreater is perceived as the mistreated. The mistreated is perceived as mistreating. There is a defensive displacement of attention to an interpersonal melodrama. The individual escapes from the arena of dramatic confrontation with a difficult reality that is experienced as more complex and dynamic than he is used to handling. The acting of the interpersonal defense perpetuates his failure to transcend and, at the same time, destroys any chance for intimacy because of the constant making or receiving of melodramatic personal attacks. The defense has put him well on his way to a daymare.

The central issue of therapy becomes the transformation of utopian personal choices, out of the individual's reach and control into viable objective options that involve the fulfillment of meaningful daydreams. Inner dreams are negotiated with outer reality. Possibilities and probabilities are reframed, analyzed, and augmented, being converted into realized daydreams. The individual must be able to evaluate inner desire as well as external options as to respective costs, risks, and gains. He must be able to generate new options, perceive existent opportunities, and act upon these for dream fulfillment. The potential relationship of the individual to his environment is optimized in terms of his innermost dreams. This therapeutic negotiation between dreams and reality takes into account the individual's most intimate desires for personal transcendence and meaningful togetherness.

In the field of psychology, the notion of a "paradigm" (Kuhn 1972) can be defined as the more or less implicit "model," conscious or unconscious, through which the person gives organization to his thoughts, feelings, and actions. It is a basic problem-solving tool through which he "frames" the picture of his relations with himself and the world. This book emphasizes the importance of analyzing and enhancing this paradigm.

To solve problems of competence it is necessary to analyze the paradigm that the person uses to address the problem. The healthy person can analyze and improve the paradigm with which he addresses problems. The emotionally unhealthy person, because of a paradigmatic rigidity and closure, is unable to meta-analyze and to improve his paradigm of understanding. This has a parallel in the ingenuous therapeutic application of a literally applied and unactualized Freudian model which, in this form, is no longer relevant to today's problems.

The first part of the book is about dreams and choices for their fulfillment. It puts forth the fundamental choice between dreams of transcending together as opposed to staying in a defensive state of illusions and delusions where the dream of transcendence is lost, provoked by the person's need to escape from anxiety. The nightmare "warning" has resulted in a defensive escape rather than in a constructive search for a solution. Meaning to life comes from the transcendent dream itself. Enthusiasm and commitment come from a realizable personal project.

The second part of the book is dedicated to actual dream fulfillment, which always encounters adversity. The emotional strength to face adversity and to resolve incompetence seems to be indispensable if the individual is to elect to pursue health rather than defend against anxiety. If he lacks emotional strength, he will make the false defensive choice and impoverish his symbolic world as well as his actual environment. He will be predisposed to mental illness, making the choice to avoid unhappiness rather than to pursue happiness. This emotional strength, fundamental to the capacity to love and to work, is developed in an historic environment of flexibility and mastery, where there is a competence in solving the inevitable problems that result from specific incompetences.

When the person has had an adequate experience of togetherness, he is able to choose the interpersonal sadomasochistic projective-introjective escape in his states of defense against anxiety. He uses his defense with the complicity of his "accomplices." He creates a "ghetto," an environment which accepts, reenforces, and assumes the necessary complementary roles to play out his personal version of the melodrama. This "melomania" allows him entry into an "indolent limbo."

When the personal melodrama fails to remove him to an indolent limbo, the individual may anesthetize himself by moving into the world of drugs or of the "telemelodrama." Here he no longer actively plays out an interpersonal projective-introjective sadomasochistic melodrama. Now he participates passively and voyeuristically in an exhibitionistic illusionary or delusional world of "teleidentifications" and telemelodramas. When this "soap opera mania" also fails to calm his anxieties, he may try drugs. His natural "endorphines" have become exhausted by the lack of commitment, hope, and meaning in his life. Artificial "morphines" become his escape.

This book looks at teleidentification with distant idealized super-"teleheroes" as a reflection of current social phenomena. Close interpersonal ties with real-life "heroes," the parents and mentors who help to establish a strong sense of personal identity and capacity to deal with a real world, have been weakened. Teleidentifications are used to obtain a voyeuristic identity through a banal, nonpersonal, and unachievable dream. Fantasy serves as a delusional escape. The teleidentification with an idealized hero is not significantly tied to a personal identity. In Freudian terms (Freud 1900), there is no "cathexis" to a personal project, which depends on a personal identity. The individual holds a dream of another's identity. He ceases to be a protagonist in his own life and escapes to a teleidentity in a telemelodrama or to drugs.

The defensive teleidentification represents a failure to generate personal dreams. A strong sense of self is absent. A hypnotic delusional state is created in which the dream of another is confused with a personal reality. This "telemelodramatic" defense is played in solitude and reflects the early solitude that provoked its development. This is in contrast to the melodramatic defense, which is played "together" with a partner and a "gang" of supporting real-life actors. This situation depends on the projection of personal qualities onto the other and the introjection of characteristics of a close other. The "melodramatic defense" is provoked by a failure to reach personal dreams through viable personal projects. The "teledefense" is based on an identification of a hypnotic sort with a larger-than-life idealized mythical hero. For example, Rita Hayworth, the "love goddess" of the forties, lived the emotional tragedy of "idealization" and "teleidentification." As a commentary on her unsuccessful attempts to find real love, and after five unhappy marriages, she once said: "Every man I knew had fallen in love with Gilda and wakened with me."

The three chapters in Part II present this paradigmatic analysis of some prototypical Manhattanite situations in which there is a loss of a personal identity. Woody Allen's *The Purple Rose of Cairo* (1985) and Judith Krantz's best-seller *I'll Take Manhattan* (1986) are used to illustrate this lonely defense. The Boesky affair of inside trading illustrates the exhibitionistic, idealized, mythical leaders who serve as "heroes" to their hypnotically fascinated mirroristic admirers.

Part III presents the active therapeutic and prophylactic construction of new choices and options for recovering and fulfilling the dream of transcendence in togetherness. The path from a masking melodrama to the true drama, from an indolent limbo to a competent lucidity, is reopened, and the upward spiral is traced to the goal of happiness. The patient's problem space is enlarged, and improvements are made in personal performance and in the environment. The emphasis is on reframing and enriching choices and options. The therapeutic relationship ought to be based on and favor a reachable transcendence in togetherness. Change starts with this patient-therapist relationship.

Part IV of the book is dedicated to the design of a preferred and viable personal project that is reachable and significant to the dream of transcendence. In this part, the specific procedures for the achievement of happiness are considered. A personal project must be tailored to the individual's most intimate dreams. The functioning of four observable variables is studied: personality style, level of abstraction in which the person tends to function, type of interpersonal authority, and politico-economic control. The combination of these four parameters produces a typology that permits the selection of therapeutic allies for the tasks of transcendence in togetherness. It allows an analysis of strengths and deficits helpful for the therapeutic reconstruction and the prophylactic construction of the relation between the patient and his macro- and microenvironment. The task is to obtain the best reachable personal choices and objective options.

The specificity with which the observable personality traits of each one of the six types is described will allow readers to readily classify their patients' as well as their own actual or potential partners, whether accomplices or allies. The choice of appropriate others offers a greater chance of success in implementing a meaningful personal project that is shared and reinforced by them.

Mariá Carmen Gear,
Ernesto César Liendo,
and Lila Lee Scott

Acknowledgments

THE AUTHORS WISH to acknowledge the vital contribution made to the writing of this book by their team of collaborators comprised of Clara Kizer, Jose Enrique Zamora, Graciela Borges, Monica Kornblith, Rocio Martinez, Esperanza Sanchez, and Jorge Posadas. As well, the book was benefited by theoretical and technical discussions with colleagues. We name the following, being aware that the list inevitably falls short of our actual debt: Carlos Featherstone, Carlos Sluzki, Alberto Eiguer, Romano Fiumara, Claudio Neri, Giorgio Corrente, Silvia Amati, Antonello Correale, Harry Prosen, Juan Miguel Hoffmann, and Stefania Manfredi.

In the multidisciplinary field we have been enriched by our contacts with the linguist Luis J. Prieto; the sociologist Daniel Glauser; the theoretical physicist Daniel Amati; the epistemologist Gregorio Klimovsky; the organizational consultant Bernardo Kliksberg; the literary critic Gloria Goldszmidt; the anthropologist Claude Levi-Strauss.

The authors also wish to recognize their personal and scientific debt to their Argentinian mentors and professors. These include Enrique Pichon-Rivière, Jose Bleger, Leon Grinberg, Mauricio Goldenberg, David Liberman, and Heinrich Racker.

On the international plane, we recognize personal orientation and supervision by Melanie Klein, Wilfred Bion, Hanna Segal, Donald Meltzer, Jacques Lacan, and Andre Green.

Finally, this book would not have been published without the ingenious and enlightening questions of our students past and present. Their candor stimulated a clarification of essential issues and from this a need to develop new answers to fulfill their desire to understand the meaning and learn the practice of a theoretically consistent and therapeutically effective multidisciplinarily enriched psychoanalysis with enhanced explanatory and operational power.

Part I

DREAMS AND OPTIONS

1

Dreams versus Illusions and Delusions

THE MOST FREQUENT reasons for psychological consultation in the United States are a crisis of anxiety, depression, or drug abuse. These symptoms reinforce one another and tend to close a pathological circle from which, over time, escape becomes difficult and often impossible. Mental health deteriorates as a sense of personal meaning, and feelings of enthusiasm and happiness diminish and disappear.

The anxiety and depression seem to depend on two fundamental and related factors: the incapacity to conceive and believe in reachable dreams of personal transcendence, and the incapacity to share dreams and their fulfillment with others. Whether the dream is actually unreachable or symbolized as such, the experience produces anxiety and depression. If dreams are believed to be unreachable, they become unrealizable. Although a belief that dreams are realizable does not necessarily make them come true, an inability to believe in a dream stops attempts to make it a reality and can lead to defensive delusions and illusions. Without the belief there is no hope, commitment, or motivation to act.

A chronic state of anxiety and, especially, a sense of failure and discouragement have physiological as well as psychological effects. These inhibit the liberation of natural endorphines that stimulate the diencephalic pleasure centers, fostering a physiological reinforcement of the psychological depression that is self-perpetuating. The person suffers a reduction in energy and the related drive to pursue daydreams.

In contrast, a hope of fulfillment of the personal dream of transcendence stimulates an enthusiastic commitment. This, in turn, stimulates the liberation of endorphines, the naturally stimulating neurotransmittors. There is a consequent increase in drive and energy—what Freud (1923) would refer to as cathecting of the object by the biologically cathected id. This energy is available for the efforts involved in dream fulfillment.

The therapeutic task is to break the downward spiral of impotence, anxiety, depression, inhibition of endorphines, lack of commitment, and feelings of helplessness in order to enter into the upward spiral of hope, enthusiasm, happiness, commitment, and liberation of endorphines. To make this change, it is necessary to transform the unreachable dreams into reachable ones with realistic options available for their fulfillment. The reachable dream must not suffer a transformation into mediocrity devoid of transcendent significance.

Emotional Escapism

One of the principal obstacles to this change from a downward spiral into an upward path is the inclination to escape from anxiety and depression, or from the warning nightmare into an emotional "addiction" which gives an immediate relief. We define "addiction" as compulsive "escapism." The individual leaves the transcendent dream. The person replaces significant interpersonal attachment and commitment to a transcendent dream with an addiction to a "pseudodream" that does not require consideration of reality factors.

This compulsive need for emotional "escapism," where the individual avoids the real challenges, detracts from his capacity to resolve real problems and anxieties. The depression increases and can cause a biological, not just a symbolic, addiction. When these psychological escape mechanisms are no longer effective, the person requires artificial "morphines," whatever their actual chemical composition. The natural endorphines are replaced by artificial exogenous "morphines" or "exorphines."

The endorphines have a cause and effect relationship to reachable dreams of transcendence in togetherness. The "morphines" serve as a cause and an effect on the defensive pseudodreams that make intimacy impossible and contribute to loneliness and isolation. The person no longer dreams to live but simply survives by way of escape into pseudodreams. The word "morphine" is derived from Morpheus, the god of sleep. The individual, under the influence of "morphine," falls into an artificial dream state. He escapes anxiety, his nightmare, and his "daymare," but has become anesthetized rather than genuinely inspired.

A psychological dose of "morphine"—which, eventually, might be reenforced by biological morphines—reduces pain, but also masks the problem. Concentration and behavior are on these stereotyped interpersonal relations. The defensive illusory "dream" is peopled by actors who blame and devalue in what becomes an illusory sadomasochistic game. All are victims and, at the same time, accomplices in a chronic mistreatment. They misread their own personal identity and stereotype affect responses. The fascination and the psychological addiction to the melodrama remove the actors from the dream of transcendencing together. They can no longer produce and share happiness. Trapped in an inevitable interpersonal unhappiness, they resign themselves to distribute this unfairly.

According to Freud (1926), the "signal anxiety" that alerts a person to the problem that must be solved to obtain happiness has been converted into "traumatic anxiety." The traumatic anxiety is then addressed as if it were the problem. A signal that something is wrong becomes so unbearable as to have to be dealt with defensively. Alarm at the problem is converted into a problem of alarm.

The search for happiness with others is abandoned in favor of a lonely flight from unhappiness. This implies a crucial switch in motivation. There is, in Freud's (1918) terms, a "perversion" in the structure of dreams and desires. The desire to seek happiness has been perverted into a desire to escape from overwhelming unhappiness. Instead of dedicating oneself to resolve the problems that impede the production of happiness, the person avoids the anxiety that the problems provoke. This would be analogous to a shopkeeper who installs a burglar alarm but finds that he is so sensitive to the noise it makes that he turns it off. He now has no immediate discomfort but gives up the warning system, which is rendered inoperative. He loses the potential for early awareness of a problem. A continual defensive escape from the perception of a painful reality exposes the person to severe reality shocks from problems that have been left to grow out of control. The nightmare warning of increasing anxiety has not been heeded. The daymare living of a chaotic reality or of the most feared situations has been allowed to occur.

The Defensive Ghetto

Defensively, the subject seeks a pseudotogetherness. Instead of seeking the company of a resolutive "command group" to face the problems that impede transcendence, he surrounds himself with a defensive "ghetto" in which his dishonest game to escape anxiety will find willing players. He looks for accepting others on whom to impose an unfair share of displeasure. Although accompanied, he is isolated from intimacy and surrounded by willing accomplices rather than helpful allies.

The group of accomplices constitute a social "morphine" or a socially shared addiction. They give a social reinforcement to the personal psychological addiction to the melodrama. This combination of a mutual reinforcement between the personal biological and psychological morphines, and the social escape mechanisms—or social morphines—constitutes a formidable resistance to the qualitative changes necessary to recover mental health. The psychological addiction to the trivial melodrama impedes commitment to the dream of transcendence. In the same way, the social addiction impedes an effective social commitment to a helpful and meaningful togetherness.

We propose that the reversion from an unhealthy addiction to a healthy commitment is possible through the psychoanalytic process based on realistic therapeutic projects and goals. The process includes the development of a meaningful and transcendent relationship between therapist and patient. Unfortunately, what often occurs is the development of a "psychoaddiction" or "psychodialysis" based on illusory or delusional therapeutic projects and goals. Another relationship of loneliness and lack of intimacy is established, this time the therapeutic relationship. Even in therapy, legitimate dreams are sabotaged by defensive illusions and delusions. Here the therapist functions as one who accompanies the patient in his anxiety but does not help to resolve its cause.

2

Choosing to Transcend Together

THIS CHAPTER DEFINES what it is to be successful in life. Although frequently envied, economic power symbolized by images of Wall Street becomes a source of happiness only when put at the service of dream fulfillment. The personal dream of transcendence and the sharing of the fruits of fulfillment — "eating the Big Apple together" — are the two ingredients of joyful living.

All organizations set objectives. The success of any enterprise is determined by the degree of correspondence of objectives and achievements. One of the principal objectives in the common "business of living" is to produce and fairly distribute a maximum of happiness and a minimum of unhappiness. A life that does not produce happiness for self and others is a failure. A person who does not dream of achievement to share with others lives without reason or purpose. The search for happiness is a basis for intimacy in the business of life.

Mental health is defined as the tendency to face and solve the problems confronted in the search for the fulfillment of meaningful dreams of shared transcendence. It depends on the ability to produce and distribute happiness. Mental illness is manifested in the tendency to produce and distribute unhappiness.

The production of happiness depends on the fulfillment of at least two convergent dreams: the dream of transcendence and the dream of sharing this with others. Integrating both dreams, we would have the dream of "shared transcendence." A "triangle of happiness" is formed by three elements: self, other, and the personal project of transcendence. Self and other are united by a considerate, valuing, and helpful relationship. They share the fruits of the personal project of transcendence.

For Freud (1900), dreams are realizations—hallucinatory, illusory, or real—of man's infantile wishes. From these dreams experienced in early infancy, the individual forms the intimate nucleus of his "psychic reality" (Freud, 1900). From them, he structures his identity and integrates his personality.

The meaning of one's psychological life would be directly linked to the fulfillment of one's most intimate wishes—the personal dreams. Their fulfillment would give a maximum state of pleasure, while their frustration provokes emotional suffering. These affect states would be the compass orienting the critical aspects of emotional life. Their absence reduces motivation and meaning in life.

Well-being does not result from the fulfillment of just any dream. "Defensive" dreams, based on illusions or delusions, temporarily calm anxiety and unhappiness but do not eventuate happiness. For dream fulfillment to produce happiness, it should be of personal transcendence shared with important others.

Transcendence

To transcend means to go beyond previous limits. It has two aspects to its definition: "trans-ascend" and "trans-scend." "Trans-ascend" means to go above what one already is, toward what one would like to become, a self-realization. It is to ascend toward the "ideal of the ego," as Freud described it. "Trans-scend" is to go beyond the limits of oneself into a full and sharing communciation with others, closing the gap between one and another.

Ideally we dream of going toward the potential best that we have in us, and of sharing this with others also capable of trans-ascending and trans-scending. Significant togetherness is not limited to sharing the same personal project. In intimately shared lives, the personal projects themselves have individual and personal flavors. This diversity enhances the lives of those who share. For example, someone who wishes to trans-ascend through contributing to scientific investigations may happily share with another who is dedicated to a career in finance. These "negotiated" differences in personal projects constitute a good base for a solid togetherness. The different interests and strengths brought to the projects for trans-ascendence reinforce the value of togetherness.

Both dreams in the triangle of happiness are of equal value. The fulfillment of one is not complete without the fulfillment of the other. Without a personal project of significant self-development, togetherness may become progressively impoverished. This may terminate in a loss of intimacy. The reverse may also occur when a couple with ambitious personal projects does not share a mutual enthusiasm and a complementary support. This dyad could lose the reason for its existence together and disappear as a couple. The personal projects could lose their significance and fail, or there could be a personal achievement but an interpersonal loneliness.

The symbolic intrapsychic capacity to plan concretely and to generate dreams of transcendence and togetherness is a necessary precondition to their fulfillment. The person must be able to imagine a personal and meaningful transcendence in a state of togetherness. The power of imagination precedes and presides over the power to do. The creative dream precedes the creative act and then what is imagined is acted upon. Making dreams real is a further stimulus to the imagination of the dreamer.

According to Freud (1923), the relationship that the individual constructs between his "Ego" and his "Ideal of the Ego" allows for the development of this capacity for symbolic transcendence. This occurs in early infancy, when the child establishes that important relationship between what he imagines he is and what he imagines that he desires and has the resources to be. The capacity for symbolic togetherness depends on the intrapsychic relation established between the "Ego" and the "Ideal Other." This determines how the individual perceives himself and whom he perceives as the ideal partner for sharing his dreams. The symbolic togetherness also rests on the intrapsychic relation between the person's "Ego" and an understanding of the "Ideal of the Ego" of this ideal other. The individual uses his symbolic capacity to imagine, understand, and help the other in the fulfillment of his dreams of personal transcendence. Lacan (1960) comments that the "desire for the other" is less significant than to "desire the desire of the other." The simultaneous desire to share the other's transcendent dream is of equal importance to that of sharing one's own transcendence with a determined type of significant other.

Symbolic Togetherness

Symbolic togetherness implies the possibilities of giving and receiving mutual understanding and help. As will be discussed later, the creation and development of the symbolic potential of the patient and significant others constitute a basic objective in the therapeutic work that enables a solid bonding.

Symbolic togetherness is the capacity for intrapsychic interaction with the representations of others who have the capacity to do the same. It fosters the development of intimacy in the couple relation, the family, and friendships. Its absence produces a profound aloneness. It makes possible a corporal togetherness and even a "teletogetherness," in which the person is accompanied "intimately," even from a physical distance. Letters, phone calls, and occasional visits keep the individual in close touch with his "preferred partners."

It is possible to feel an intimate togetherness with Verdi, when hearing his music; or with Picasso, when seeing his art; or with Einstein, when studying his theories. These experiences provoke the pleasure of intimacy when they can be shared with another with the same level of symbolic elaboration. This capacity for symbolic togetherness implies a capacity for a symbolic "togetherness with the self." The subject enjoys a self-supporting relation of transcendence with his own self-image. He likes and believes in himself and supports himself in his own efforts, which he perceives as important and valuable.

Let us imagine a situation where a unique being was sad after death, although he had reached paradise. He had received this reward because of his extreme goodness. Since he was the only good person on earth, he was the sole inhabitant of paradise. All the others were more or less "happily" enjoying their inferno. At one point the crowd in hell asked him just why he was so sad in spite of his enviable environment. He replied that he envied their possibility of sharing their suffering. He said, "Although I have everything, with whom do I share it?" This is the plight of some millionaires who have everything materially but are never "loved for themselves," only "for their money."

Romanticism or Melodrama

The concepts of transcendence and of togetherness, as what gives sense to the "business of life," need to include the distinction between "romanticism" and "melodramatism," which are often linked together and confused. They have fundamental differences. Romanticism favors a meaningful transcendence in togetherness. Melodramatism sabotages both transcendence and togetherness in a way which is difficult to modify, because the melodrama is a subtle—or not subtle—caricature of togetherness. Romanticism leads to a constructive emotional attachment. Melodramatism leads to an emotional addiction and isolation.

Romanticism implies a willingness to overcome any obstacle and to confront limitless suffering in order to transcend together. Any price is worth paying to reach this transcendence in togetherness. In melodramatism, the person is willing to pay the cost of happiness only up to a point. There is the belief that transcendence and togetherness are too costly and, as a result, somehow unachievable. The person carefully measures his efforts and consoles himself with trivialities in a shared loneliness. He neither trans-ascends nor trans-scends.

Transcendence and the emotional comfort of the "easy life" seem to be incompatible. Looking to play it safe and easy leads to a state of "no pains and no gains." The melodramatist is satisfied with banality. The drama of life passes him by. He hoards his means and does not value ends. His life plays out like a soap opera, where pseudoemotions occupy center stage.

If there is to be a belief and hope, the dream has to be transformable into realistic projects. The means must be perceived as enough to achieve the ends. The person must experience the probability of being able to fulfill his dreams if he is willing to pay the cost and make the heroic effort. This state of probability is what feeds his enthusiasm. He is already symbolically transcending in togetherness. He can see how it can be done. This reinforces commitment and stimulates endorphines, providing greater energy resources for the project's achievement.

The Sense of Happiness

To create the sense of happiness, the dream must be a deep and personal expression of the historic "Ideal of the Ego." The dream must be negotiated with the current reality, but the principle of the dream must not be lost, or the sense of transcendence is lost. The dream may be negotiated but must not be perverted into a defensive melodrama. When it is forcefully or voluntarily renounced, there is a risk of the avoidant addiction to the melodrama. Retaining the dream and the personal project is indispensable. Neither transcendence nor togetherness is negotiable.

Happiness is an intense and full experience of psychological ecstasy. It is the emotion of being in the goal state. Enthusiasm for life is a part of the process of "becoming," in contrast to the state of "arriving." Enthusiasm and satisfaction are more enduring and are frequent daily emotions that keep us going between the rarer states of ecstasy. Satisfaction is experienced in the process of working toward the goal and being "on task" with a project which leads to a better self. As well, there is a satisfaction with having supporting intimate others who also believe in our dreams. Meaning, enthusiasm, and happiness, which depend on dreams, projects, and fulfillment, reinforce one another.

The word *enthusiasm* comes from the Greek "en-theos" or "to be with God." The notion of "being with God" could be reformulated as the long-cherished human dream of transcending the mortal condition. To have enthusiasm—"to be with God"— means having a reachable dream and a viable transcendent project—not necessarily mystical or religious, but philosophically transcendent—which represents the best potential being that resides within us. It is the belief that we will be able to transcend, to "go beyond our present condition," in spite of the costs, difficulties, and frustrations of daily life. A progressive depression would set in, and the enthusiastic commitment in the search for happiness would give way to a concentration on avoiding unhappiness. Addiction to escapism and a refusal to pay the cost of self-actualization leave the individual in a void.

The use of abstract romantic terms such as happiness, enthusiasm, and solidarity does not imply that these ideas are vague. They are well defined and are brought to action. It is this romanticism, well applied, that makes daily life possible. Just as we accept that there is "noting more practical than a good theory" (Lewin 1966), there is nothing more realistic than an applicable romanticism, and nothing more romantic than a good realism. As Sartre (1968) points out, only the power of imagination can bring imagination to power. The romanticism of dreaming is linked to the realism of fulfilling dreams through viable projects of transcendence in togetherness. Romanticism, then, is not a utopian expression, but rather a realistic expression of what could be if we try. It is a romanticism in practice. In this way, we can overcome the Aristotelian dilemma between being a "utopian reformer" or a "cynical conservative." There is an enthusiastic bonding with reality. The subject is neither lost in unachievable dreams nor lost in cynical and bitter reality.

The therapeutic process needs to be a living experience of the marriage of romanticism with realism. Therapists must be able to dream meaningful and reachable therapeutic dreams, and create viable therapeutic projects that are effectively implemented in therapeutic action plans. They must take into account, and use, the maximum resources available to themselves, their patients, and their environment, and not settle for less than the best possible effort.

3

Early Signs of Emotional Incompetence

TO ACHIEVE A shared happiness, competence in two areas is essential: in the politico-economic world of project fulfillment and in the world of interpersonal intimacy. The possibility to conceive these reachable dreams and to undertake viable projects with enthusiasm, commitment and drive depends on intellectual, emotional, social, and physical competence. This competence is required in order to take advantage of the available means — actual or potential — to reach the transcendent goal in a state of meaningful togetherness. To have a "competent mind" for the person's intimate and specific concerns, is a necessary, although not the sole, condition for the mastery of the inner and outer worlds. The person creates a realistic relationship between the means at his disposal and his own personal transcendent ends, in order to search for them enthusiastically while he is supported in this search by understanding and caring others.

When there is incompetence, it would be healthy to deal with and attempt to overcome the specific intellectual, emotional, social, and/or physiological deficits. The mentally ill, or "incompetent of mind," have a psychological avoidant addiction when faced with these deficits. When they experience a warning nightmare or live a daymare, they escape to a voyeuristic teleidentification or an interpersonal projective and introjective sadomasochistic melodrama. If means appear to be lacking to reach the personal transcendent goal, this defensive attitude further widens the gap and makes the unreachableness of the dream a certainty. The mentally ill abandon and do not enter the search for solutions.

The healthy individual responds competently when faced

with his and the environment's incompetence. The disturbed person reacts incompetently when faced with his own incompetence. Since we all suffer some degree of incompetence, it is not the simple incompetence that is the mark of mental illness. The type of response to the incompetence is the key for differentiation. The "competent mind" can resolve the problems that obstruct the goal, creating the options needed for transcendent dream fulfillment. The mentally unhealthy are meta-incompetent. They cannot address problems in general. They could be said to be lacking in the capacity for "reverie" (Bion 1962); that is, the capacity to sufficiently contain their anxiety in order to be able to explore and elaborate it intelligently.

Social and Interpersonal Incompetence

The incompetent mind further complicates problems with a tendency to select and construct an equally incompetent environment that does not offer the options necessary to implement a viable project for transcendent dream fulfillment. The downward spiral toward depression and anxiety is reinforced.

We will distinguish two forms of incompetence: the "phallic" type, in the area of social power, and the personal type, which demands a strong sense of self as a prerequisite for a personally cathected dream and potential for intimacy. We will try to define the childhood environmental conditions that contribute to incompetence.

Family Life in Freud's Time

Early childhood and sociocultural environments have changed radically since Freud's nineteenth-century Vienna. If Freud were to visit Manhattan now, one might imagine what he would identify as the problems of growing up and the causes of emotional weaknesses. Which would he view as the fundamental variables producing mental disturbances? Sexual repression and women confined to roles of dependence without social power were typical of his century. Hysteria was then as common a disease as depression and drug addiction are today. Lack of intimacy seemed to be related to the repression of sexual impulses. In today's Manhattan, he might establish a different set of "givens," or assumptions. There are fewer hysterical women, fewer women who have not discovered the enjoyment of their own bodies or are unable to acknowledge their own impulses. He would, however, find a lonely crowd. Family life, sacred in Freud's lifetime, is considered a "heresy in New York" (Richards 1987), where unromantic couples live in shared loneliness. He would be confronted by this strange new form of intimacy, an instant, uncompromised, and uncommited "intimacy." He might postulate that the desperation of loneliness was being repressed through promiscuity, alcohol abuse, and teleidentifications.

Factors such as social mobility, the loss of the extended family, and a sense of rootlessness influence the sense of personal identity and capacity for intimacy. Manhattan no longer fosters family life. Working, divorced, and otherwise preoccupied parents rear "latchkey" children and are limited in what they can give to the symbolic capacity for intimacy. The parent has lost the important function of "reverie" (Bion 1960), the containing of the child's anxiety during the process of a more complete symbolic understanding of his experience. Through this "uterine" function (Gear and Liendo 1975), the child experiences the psychological closeness that inspires and builds a sense of self and autonomy. Intimacy becomes meaningful with a strong definition of self and a faith in the potential presence of a supporting and helpful other—what Feuerstein (1980) calls an "enriching mediator." This basic capacity needed for intimacy is damaged by inadequate early parenting. Parents need to contain the anxiety of the child, in his learning by trial and error. Today's child often does not have these first mentors.

Just as Spitz (1945) showed that physical contact is necessary for survival and growth, it appears that early ongoing psychological contact is a prerequisite for the development of the capacity for intimacy. If the self is diminished, a state of passivity and a need for drugs and teleidentification can result. For the child without healthy parental contact there is an impoverished ability for togetherness. The deficit that this produces is dramatic in its social effect, as was the deprivation of physical contact in Spitz's infants. This incapacity to be intimate is a common characteristic of the children of alcoholics. They cannot risk intimacy in a chaotic and unpredictable environment. They are themselves predisposed to alcoholism. Paradoxically, they are somehow trapped and condemned to the same "escape" that destroyed their parents. The incapacity for intimacy perpetuates across generations.

Identification and the Hypnotic State

When people suffer from anomie (Durkheim 1951) — a feeling of not belonging to a meaningful structure — they do not have a sense of who they are or what they personally represent. Freud (1921) referred to the phenomenon of "identification" and the hypnotic state. A loss of "identity" — or better, an identification with the loved and idealized leader who represents a mythical "Ego Ideal" (Freud 1923) — represents a form of teleidentification. Another is the giving over of identity to the "hypnotist," who takes charge of the passive other's identity. The hypnotic state is like a dream state in which one dreams the dream of the "other." These are examples of the mechanisms behind the teleidentifications and the insatiable need to know more about the "real" story of the lives of the charismatic leaders and the idealized teleheroes. Life is led through these others' lives. One's own life pales in the shadow of the hero. Freud stated that the masses idealize their leaders and identify with them similarly to the idealization of the teleheroes. In

The Purple Rose of Cairo Manhattan's own Woody Allen (1985) tragically, amusingly, and accurately portrays the problem. The heroine escapes from the real world and personal daydreams or daymares to a fantasy world, where there is a voyeuristic identification with the film's heroine and the male star of the movie steps out of the screen into the everyday life of the avid watcher. One's own identity is missing. There are no personal daydreams or sense of personal importance. It is not just that one fails in an attempt to fulfill a personal project. The problem is more basic.

From a young age, children may teleidentify with their mythical heroes, such as "Master of the Universe." Their teleidentifications are even more ambitious than those of their parents, who identify with heroes who have circumscribed goals and limitations. The power of the whole universe is theirs. What an impossible dream to convert into reality! Better to stay in fantasy land. Through the television set, one may identify with and lead the life of a larger-than-life hero. People are gratified by passively watching the celluloid fantasies of others while a personal dream becomes more distant and unattractive.

Power Envy

The parenting function has a second aspect, a phallic one of preparing children to have an optimistic and confident attitude toward politico-economic tasks, accompanied by skills learned from parental modeling and personal tutoring. This gives a politico-economic sense of "potency." When this function is not fulfilled, there is a "learned helplessness" (Seligman 1975) and hopelessness. When the phallic function occurs, there is a realistic sense of personal mastery, a faith in one's ability to act effectively with technical know-how.

Freud would face the need to reframe the "castration complex" and to confront what is repressed. Let us imagine what would inevitably occur to him walking along Fifth Avenue. Would he have interpreted Trump Tower as a concrete erect penis being shamelessly exhibited to fill women with envy? Would his thinking have gone beyond this to the generic problem of "power envy," or social castration rather than a physical one? It is unlikely that he would have confused "penis," a sexual organ, with "phallus," a social "organ." Impotence in the face of social problems—the psychological bag people, not just the literal bag ladies of New York—would come to his attention. The importance of having the social power to survive and then to make survival worthwhile would have surely been topics of his and his colleagues' concern.

It is no longer simply that fathers proudly exhibit a sexual organ that threatens the growing child. It is the absent defeated parent who cannot retain a sense of control in his own life or aspire to his own dreams. Learned helplessness results from the feeling of being a helpless and insignificant member of the mass mind. Perhaps the impact of the American spirit of being an "Outward Bounder," of being successful in the face of adversity, is reflected in the purchasing by parents of survival training for their children. For a fee, their children leave the city to meet the challenge of nature. They are given a ready-made experience of physical survival in adversity. They experience the value of allies and intelligent altruism as the group shares the struggle to "overcome." This cooperative and demanding experience is infrequent in the competitive and personally isolating big-city life.

The disintegration of the family, the absence of support systems, the democratization—sometimes referred to as the "mediocritization" of education—cause a sense of conviction that "I can't, no matter how much I try." Problems in the way of daydream fulfillment have become more complex. Emotional resources for solving them diminish.

Two Defenses

How does this state of mind express itself in one's psychology? Common reasons for consultation in school health services hold some answers. Apathy and underachievement or drug abuse reflect problems of commitment. In adults seeking consultation, the more frequent related disorders are depression, anxiety, and drug addiction.

Two levels of defense result from a sense of anomie: an interpersonal melodramatic defense of projection and introjection, and a more primitive defense of impersonal teleidentifications. When there is a failure of the "phallic parenting"—but the "uterine parenting" is adequate—the person uses an interpersonal melodramatic defense. With a more basic failure in the development of a sense of self and personal worth, the individual becomes a nobody without an identity. He may calm existential anxiety, his daymare and his nightmare, by escaping into the world which Freud associated with the process of massification. He overidentifies with idealized superheroes and becomes a passive voyeurist hypnotically enjoying "the celluloid dreams of others," which are transmitted in a process similar to a "mass hypnotism."

The Paleoenvironment

The early environment of the mentally unhealthy did not facilitate the acquisition or problem-solving skills. It promotes a primitive, oversimplifying, and closed approach without a constructive self-criticism. Feedback is absent or biased. This historic environment, which produces meta-incompetence, will be referred to as the *paleoenvironment*. The incompetent and meta-incompetent mind that results will be termed the *paleomind*. This paleomind, in its incompetent reactions, tends to be narrow and rigid. The healthy, competent, and resolutive equivalent of the paleomind will be called the *neomind*—produced in a *neoenvironment*—which is broad, complex, flexible, and capable of a constructive critical approach to problems. A competent neomind predisposes to the conception and fulfillment of reachable transcendent dreams in togetherness. In contrast, the paleomind predisposes to the melodrama and its consequent unhappiness, within an incompetent paleoenvironment.

Mental illness manifests when the incompetent paleomind is obliged to confront sharp qualitative changes in self and/or environment. New and significantly different problems have to be coped with and solved. The paleomind insists, counterproductively, in offering the old, and now irrelevant, solutions. He tries to understand new problems as if these were the same old ones. As a result, there is failure, the situation becomes catastrophic, and a daymare is experienced. The paleomind enters into a critical incompetence. This is a crisis of meta-incompetence, since the person is unable to meta-analyze what is wrong with how he is trying to solve the problem, and this adds to the sense of failure.

The incompetence to solve problems may be predominantly intellectual, emotional, social, and/or physical. The meta-failure to address the problem of how to solve problems depends strongly on a specific emotional incompetence, a failure to contain the traumatic anxiety. This emotional incapacity does not allow the person to reduce the anxiety enough to revert it to a signal level (Freud 1926). The person is overwhelmed and unable to persist in a positive confrontation with the stressor. He defends against anxiety rather than dealing with the original source of anxiety.

Unfortunately, contemporary society offers continuous confrontations between the complex changing new world and the simplistic static paleomind (Toffler 1980). The adult individual was psychologically prepared to deal with a world that no longer exists. The present is unlike the past. We could say that "the future is no longer what it used to be" and the individual must meet "culture shocks." If he continues to offer obsolete solutions to new problems, he will fall into "terrible simplifications" (Watzlawick 1974). The paleomind, with its rigid conceptions, does not admit corrective self-criticism. It is unsuited to a changing world. Finally, the individual cannot learn from past experience or readily recognize and correct his own errors. There is a distortion, often irreversible, between the paleophrenic structure of the mind and the neostructure of the world.

Part II

FALSE OPTIONS

4

Choosing to Avoid Anxiety through Melodrama

THE CONSCIOUS OR unconscious perception of the limitations of the paleomind is a realization of incompetence to reach meaningful dreams. The person is lucid but perceives himself as powerless to change his reality. This awareness confirms the fear that the transcendent dream is unachievable.

The paleomind is a narrow inadequate frame from which problems are approached and reality experienced. The individual is not able to alter the discrepancy between the available means and the ends to be achieved. He cannot reframe or add to his choices or objective options.

This perception of an unresolvable incompetence is consolidated in what Freud (1915c) terms "the castration complex." Doubt becomes certainty about the unreachableness of the transcendent dream. Seligman (1975), in another context, called this "learned helplessness."

The continued and repeated failure of the paleomind leads to emotional pain with increasing anxiety, demoralization, hopelessness, and apathy with a decreasing commitment and a reduction in the endorphines. The point is reached where there is no drive toward transcendence in togetherness and the only remaining option is a desperate escape to an indolent limbo. A defensive illusional or delusional parallel world is created, and the person gradually distances himself from the painful reality (Neri 1983). This is a crucial moment in that it changes the meaning and purpose of life. The goal has changed. There is a switch from the constructive search for happiness to a defensive escape from unhappiness into a fool's paradise.

This fool's paradise is indolent in two senses of the word: it is both passive and "in-dolent," without pain. The defense is against the psychic pain produced by an awareness of personal incompetence and failure in what is vital to happiness, or against an awareness of solitude. The defensive response to this situation adopts a popular and universal form. The person must enter an illusional and sometimes delusional melodramatic world, a defensive parareality (Watzlawick 1976), created by a paraphrenic mind. With time he becomes even more removed from reality and more trapped in a defensive parareality.

Defensive Avoidance

The melodramatic necessity is a product of a censorship that represses the perception of the relevant drama. Attention is systematically displaced from the dramatic failure to fulfill the transcendent desire. Dramatic desire hits a censorship and is deviated, being displaced toward the melodramatic necessity to avoid anxiety. From this moment the interest of the subject is evasive. This displacement is possible as a result of the previous repression of the relevant drama accompanied by an intolerant anxiety produced by consciousness of a vital failure. The melodrama is irrelevant and, in a certain sense, an anxiolytic.

Many years of clinical observation in psychotherapy indicate that the use of the melodrama is a more or less universal defense mechanism. It is a response to the feeling that one is not able to fulfill the transcendent dream of togetherness. In modern times, the togetherness aspect has become as problematic as was transcendence during the Depression. This is reflected in the popularity of voyeuristic teleidentifications of melodramatic novels. The personally created and interpersonally acted defensive melodrama becomes more difficult to act as groups of individuals join the undifferentiated masses of people.

Melodrama

Melodrama literally means "to be addicted to drama." It is, in fact, a perversion of the drama. The melodrama, as a theatrical form, exaggerates the sentimental aspects of the drama. It distorts what is essential to romanticism. It is a caricature of the romantic's sensibility to transcendence. Drama is replaced by farce. There are few things more antiromantic than a melodrama (Therive 1965).

It appears that the "soap," the television series dedicated to sentimentalism, the "make 'em laugh, make 'em cry" (Reed 1987) programs have strong appeal to a significant number of the population. Thirty million Britons watch "Eastenders." Fifty million Americans watch their favorite version of the packaged melodrama. The Japanese view "Machigai-darake no Onna-migaki."

The melodrama has been termed the "anti-novel" without the foundations of the human drama. Drama deals with transcendence and togetherness, both in the tragic sense and in the sense of fulfillment. The melodrama is a type of paraliterature, artificial and nonauthentic. It is the "soap opera," the "dime novel," the "counter novel," the "kitchen novel," the "roman pour biblioteque de gare," "roman pour concierge," "telenovela" and so on. Real-life conditions are replaced by pseudodrama, in which millionaires are married for money and destroy one another in a lust for power, are unlucky in love, and in general epitomize absolutely unenviable personal lives. Or the theme is the past, when things were difficult but the hero "overcame" by simply struggling harder. He knew who he was and what he could do. He had the emotional strengths to go for it against all odds. There was hope. In others a family with remote unimaginable frustrations and crises with their children stick together and overcome. The formula of required suffering and sacrifice is experienced as a family.

Telemelodrama

There are many sociological explanations for this phenomenon. An individual melodrama is personal. It has complementary actors who share the person's universe, and a real group, or "ghetto," which shares the fundamental perceptions and values of the actors. The plot is melodramatic. The personal melodrama is based on complementary projections and introjections between real partners who share an environment of friends and family. This defense has given way to the teleidentification with "soaps." The interpersonal melodrama is a defense against a failure to fulfill dreams of transcendence, where there is some semblance of sadomasochistic bonding and "togetherness" in the web of their lives. The teleidentification is available to those who are even more lonely and equally impotent to change their reality in terms of togetherness or of transcendence. They use the mechanism of "idealization" (Freud 1923) of a distant and mythical hero who overcomes in the face of the most difficult circumstances. Their own "inferior" identity is lost hypnotically, as they identify with the superhero. Their lack of a family and their diminishing sense of a personally significant self are defended against by a vicarious voyeurism. They have someone to care for and to worry about. They have a T.V. "family." Their envy of more fortunate others who live happily in families without problems is assuaged by this peek at family life. Here, too, the protagonists suffer at the hands of "bad" others.

Both defenses, the telemelodrama and the interpersonal melodrama, foster mediocrity. They focus attention on the melodrama, which deviates from the need to address and resolve a real dramatic problem of life, be it politico-economic or interpersonal. The person can participate voyeuristically and passively although alone and avoid the pain of the daymare as best he can.

The telemelodrama appears to violate rules of good writing in order to retain the interest of the reader who is looking for escapism. We must remember that the melodrama has been defined in another context as dreaming with the eyes open; that is, as a certain type of delusion or hallucination. In order to achieve this evasive illusion, history, truth, ideology, and even logic are subordinated (Bory 1960). The reader wants easy access to the anecdote. The melodrama simplifies the representations of good and bad. Its moral code idealizes masochism as an innocent altruism. It condemns sadism, which is portrayed as astute and malintentioned egoism.

The melodrama loses its aesthetic sense because it relies on anecdote to mask the real story. It is designed to allow flight from one's own authentic drama. It is a distortion of reality destined for the "retarded." It is an escape from the opera of life to the "soap opera of pseudolife" (Ganny 1966).

By way of the melodrama the person avoids intolerable perceptions of the unreachableness of a meaningful transcendence in togetherness. In Freudian terms (Freud 1915b), the real dreams are repressed and replaced. When the person is resigned to his castration and an acceptance that he cannot reach the dream of a shared transcendence, he tries the melodramatic escape to a pseudotranscendence in a false togetherness. He escapes from life's realistic drama—the "opera of life"—toward an unrealistic melodrama—the "soap opera of living."

Desire and Instinct

It could be useful here to link the two types of desires or dreams, the fulfillment of which brings happiness, to the two instincts that were postulated by Freud (1915c) in his first classification of them. The desire for togetherness is derived from the "sexual instinct," the desire for transcendence from the "self-preservation instinct." It is possible to attempt to fulfill these desires, paying the unavoidable price of a dose of inevitable but tolerable anxiety implicit in this process. Or the individual could attempt to escape from the high price that he perceives these desires demand. In terms of the second classification of the instincts, the "life instinct" and the "death instinct," postulated by Freud (1920), when the person seeks happiness, although conscious of the high emotional price that is involved, the life instinct predominates. When the decision is to defend against the high price, the death instinct prevails. At times, the desire for togetherness competes with the desire for transcendence. At other times, these reinforce one another.

If the desire for togetherness depends on the sex instinct and the desire for transcendence derives from the self-preservation instinct, the search or motivation to fulfill both would depend on the life instinct. Not to fulfill these would be linked to the death instinct. It is important to maintain balance and integrate the sex instinct with the self-preservation instinct. A predominance of the first would lead to a hypertrophy of the seeking of togetherness and an atrophy of the seeking of transcendence. A predominance of the second would lead to a hypertrophy of the seeking of transcendence and an atrophy of the seeking of togetherness. When the two instincts are in harmony, a constructive life instinct predominates over the death instinct.

5

Defensive Monothematic Inverted Speech

THE NEED TO defend oneself from anxiety can predispose to a strong addiction to the melodrama. The melodrama itself could be considered an addiction to sentimentalism. This "meloaddiction" reaches the proportions of a "melomania" and seems to become the preferred defense mechanism. The person can deny the painful recognition of incompetence in producing happiness. Instead of dealing metacompetently with his own incompetence, the energy is employed to avoid or reduce anxiety at the cost of lucidity and sensibility. The emotionally incompetent displaces attention (Freud 1915b) unconsciously and compulsively. He substitutes the tasks of dream fulfillment for melodrama. Although counterproductive to the development of feelings of happiness, it serves temporarily to calm anxieties and depression. This defensive solution perpetuates the original critical problem. There is, according to Freud (1915b), a "return of the repressed" in spite of the defense. From time to time, the person becomes conscious of the increasing discomfort of his psychic reality. He becomes ever more helpless, hopeless, and anxious. There is no sense of mastery.

The protagonists of this escapist melodrama are of two classes (Gear and Liendo 1981). There are sadistic, astute victimizers who, by mechanisms of "projection" and "introjection," perceive and describe themselves as masochistic victims while acting as victimizers. Complementarily, there are masochistic victims who perceive and describe themselves as sadistic, astute victimizers while being victims. The sadists see themselves as masochists as they morally and intellectually disqualify the others in a stereotyped transaction. They accuse the masochists of being "bad," "foolish," or "crazy." The masochists accept and reinforce these disqualifications and overqualify the accusing sadists as "good," "intelligent," and "sensible" (Freud 1924b). In Freudian terms, the sadists project their sadism onto the masochists while introjecting the masochism. The masochists project their masochism onto the sadists and introject sadism. Both are victims of the melodrama. The game is endless and without gain or winners. To play is to lose the possibility of pursuing happiness in the transcendent dream of togetherness. The sadists, who treat their friends like enemies, are not morally "bad." The masochists, who treat their enemies like friends, are not morally "good." Sartre (1960) would refer to them as "semivictims and semiaccomplices" in a melodramatic game played by many but won by none.

Sadomasochistic Complicity

Paradoxically, the sadist and the masochist join forces and denounce any outsider who attempts to interrupt and help to end the game. They act as if their "worst enemy" is the one who tries to shed the light of resolutive intelligence on the game.

This inversion of what is said and what the participants of the melodramatic sadomasochistic game do results, in part, from a social ethic learned in their early paleoenvironment. There is a contradiction between the sanctioned formal "norms" and the unsanctioned informal "rules" (Levi-Strauss 1949), which must be followed to be rewarded. The existence of this contradiction is denied. The norms support the masochist in his "altruism," but the pragmatic rules of the game reward the egocentric sadist. The sadomasochistic ethic based on egocentrism was encouraged in the paleoenvironment. Its objective is to unfairly distribute unhappiness between the players. The rules and meta-rules impede the game of transcendence in togetherness. The game is self-defeating, because it further undermines the ability to achieve what is most desired.

The incompetent paleomind that evolves out of the paleoenvironment is an integral factor in the creation of the "melomind." Although incompetent to produce happiness, it can utilize some means at its disposal to handle the anxiety and depression that come from incompetence to produce happiness. It is able to establish a "meloenvironment" similar to the original paleoenvironment. In a defensive illusion the melodramatist evades problems and recruits others to follow this pattern. Together, they experience an indolent limbo in a parareality. Here there is little sharing. All are protected from critical lucidity until a new wave of "reality shocks" shakes the defenses and produces more emotional suffering.

The sadist seeks to make the other suffer displeasure. The masochist absorbs this unhappiness and gives priority to avoiding psychic pain. The irrelevant anxieties of the melodrama are preferred to the anxieties of failure in the drama. In the melodramatic escape there is a repression of the "true" dreams, which are perceived as beyond realization. Attention is displaced and fixed on the "melodream," or melodramatic pseudodream.

Projective Identification

Within the melodream, the sadism or masochism is projected onto the other. The sadist feels mistreated by the masochist. The emotional incompetence compels the person to think, speak, and act in reverse. He reiterates the theme of mistreatment that is his melodrama. His thought is monothematic about victimization. The actors may differ, but the play is the same (Eco 1966). The relationship of mistreatment repeats with the same sequence and inverted perception. This is what Levi-Strauss (1949) referred to as "the eternal return of the same," and what Freud (1909b) called the "repetition compulsion." This is determined by the defensive melomind, addicted to melosadism and melomasochism. The characters act within a reliable defensive meloenvironment, or melodramatic "ghetto." The personal melodramatic repetition compulsion of auto- and heterodestruction is either sadistic or masochistic. When the sadist confronts a personal failure, there is a determined offensive and aggressive response pattern against others. The masochist, in the same circumstances, would react by accepting the offensive aggression. Each person tends to assume a position that is predominantly sadistic or masochistic. At some time, the sadist may confront the need to play his game when there is only another more powerful sadist available. Here, he must invert roles and temporarily cast himself as the masochist in the same sadomasochistic melodrama. The need to invert the roles may also occur for the melomasochist. The roles remain counterproductive and block happiness, transcendence, or togetherness.

The intrapsychic obsession with the melodrama is an interpersonal melodramatic behavioral compulsion. Each of the principal complementary actors induces the role of the melodramatic accomplice in his unconsciously but carefully selected partner. They are accomplices in this game of devaluing and blaming, which occurs whenever there is a crisis of incompetence. As well, they form a melodramatic chorus that expresses a pathogenic agreement to focus on melodramatic personalized mistreatment, and to identify and talk about it "in reverse." The individual and his "ghetto" abandon their attempts at resolutive productive action and are trapped in the defensive melodramatic interplay. Asch (1956) shows how the individual unconsciously creates his own confirming "micromajority." The sadist usually instigates this and the masochist accepts it. They abandon an intelligent interpersonal interchange of intimacy and helpfulness for the interminable stereotyped interaction of interpersonal disqualification. They pass from the greatness of macrodramatic problems to the mediocrity of stereotyped micromelodramatic problems.

The selection of the melodramatic accomplices contributes to the establishment of the incompetent meloenvironment. This, in turn, contributes to, and reinforces, the incompetent meloperformance and melomind. The historic pathogenic paleoenviron-

Defensive Monothematic Inverted Speech

ment has been reproduced. This environment, in turn, reinforces the compulsion to the melodrama. The narcissistic ghetto offers only one option: the defensive monotheme of the melodrama. It does not suggest a resolutive option or introduce new choices. There is a reduction in inner dreams and outer options, and a continuous reinforcement of this impoverishment.

When the individual falls into the melodramatic hypnotic trance, reenforced by the accomplices, he is trapped in a sadomasochistic monologue. He mentates as he is perceived and reflected in the other. He, like Narcissus, believes that he is talking to another (Fiumara 1983). He talks with his projection and introjects the identity of the other. He is "alone" in a confused identity and out of touch even with himself. Meaningful communication cannot occur. He is condemned to solitude. He may believe that he is "together" with others, but essentially he is always "alone together" (Weber 1987). The other is taken and treated as nothing more than a reflection of himself.

To understand the inverted melodramatic discourse, it is necessary to revert both the sequence and the direction of the stereotyped description of the mistreatment. To obtain what Freud (1905) called the "latent content," it is necessary to multiply the "manifest content" by minus one (-1). That is, he who believes that he is being mistreated is, in fact, mistreating. He who feels that he initiated the mistreatment has been the recipient. When the person talks about the incompetence of the other, he is projecting his own incompetence. What is repressed into the unconscious is the inverse of what is perceived in consciousness.

6

The Sadomasochistic and Narcissistic Monologue

TO THE DEGREE that the other functions as a reflecting inverting mirror, a meaningful dialogue is not possible between the characters of a melodrama. In a double complementary and mirroring "falsification" of identities, they perceive in others what they themselves are feeling or doing. Each assumes the identity of the other. Both participants speak and act in reverse.

The melodramatic escape has a certain similarity to the Freudian concept of narcissism (Freud 1914a). A transcendence into meaningful togetherness can be achieved only if the narcissism and the melodrama are resolved. Narcissism is characterized by a constricted, almost impenetrable "individualistic" melodramatic monologue that impedes or sabotages healthy communication.

In narcissism and in the melodramatic world, the person looks into a mirror to see his own sadomasochism reflected as he plays his own version of the stereotyped sadomasochistic interpersonal game. Freud (1924a) describes narcissism as a more or less impenetrable individualism with a simulated togetherness. There is a pseudocontact with mirrored images of the self. Others are used as melodramatic accomplices to escape anxiety and depression.

This painful incompetence in producing happiness is defended against. Narcissism, like the melodramatic escape, attacks clarity. Both violate the altruism necessary to produce transcendence in togetherness. Instead, they create a relationship of stereotyped, impenetrable, and sadomasochistic individualism. Even though functioning in a dyadic or polyadic context, what develops is a "shared loneliness" disguised as a "togetherness." Their world becomes a microworld of melodrama.

This melodramatic escape is the defense of the incompetent, impotent melomind derived from the primary paleoenvironment. This melomind is characterized by its tendency to narrowness and oversimplification, and by a lack of constructive self-criticism that impedes learning from new experience. Narcissism cannot produce happiness, only unhappiness.

Seven Anxiety-Avoiding Mechanisms

In the narcissistic escape, the person tends to use a series of unconscious intrapsychic defense mechanisms to avoid awareness of his castration complex (Freud 1922). Unable to reach his dream of transcendence toward his Ideal of the Ego and happiness, the person turns to escape mechanisms such as "repression," "displacement," "splitting," "projection," "introjection," "idealization," and "denigration."

As an example, a person who loses his job because he has not kept abreast of technological developments may defend from this failure. He "represses" the perception of his impaired or incomplete skills and status and "displaces" by attention to wife abuse. He "splits" melodramatic roles into those who mistreat and those who are mistreated. He mistreats his wife and "projects" onto her the felt mistreatment while "introjecting" her identity of being the one mistreated. He then "idealizes" and overqualifies himself as the superior, good husband while he "denigrates" his wife. These mechanisms are limited to a simple transitory neutralization of psychic pain. Since they do not resolve the underlying incompetence, there is a periodic "return of the repressed" awareness of the traumatic incompetence. In moments of reality testing the patient lives the daymare. (See Fig. 6-1.)

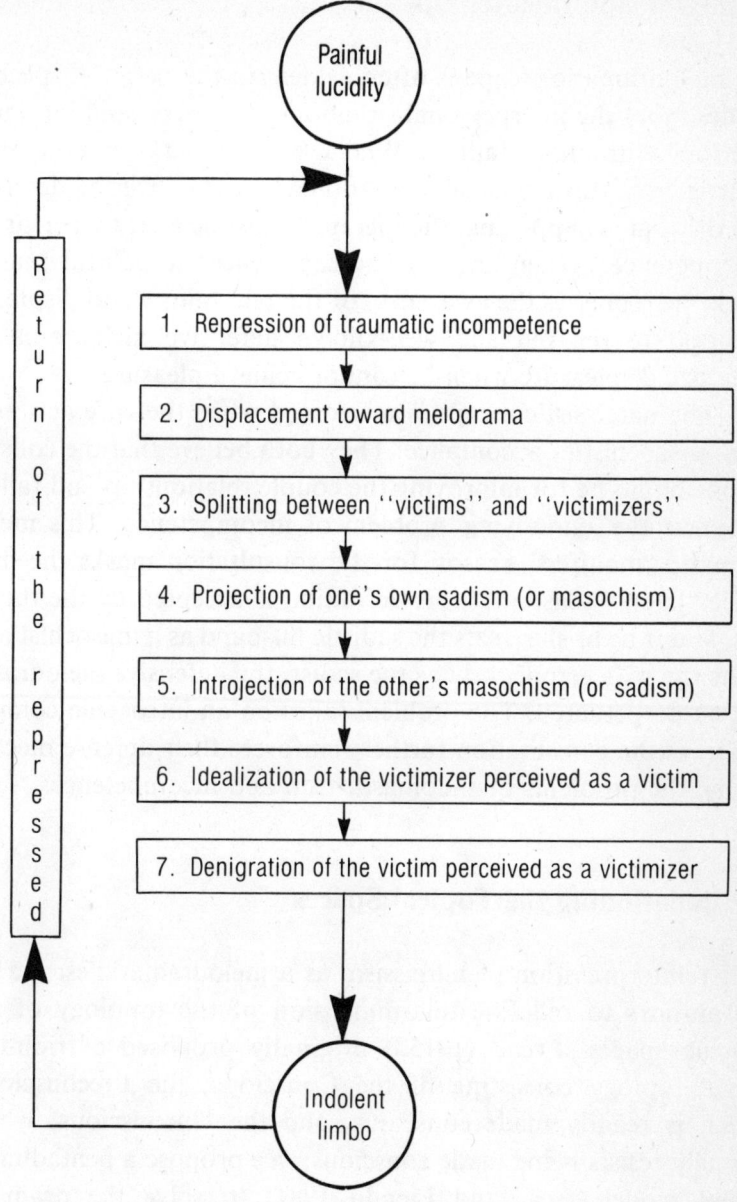

Figure 6-1 From painful lucidity to indolent limbo

Monothematic Inverted Speech

The melodramatic escape is often evident in the patient's speech. He describes the interpersonal situations in reverse, and does not mention a dramatic failure. Whenever the therapist notes the recurrence of this tendency to a sadomasochistic inverted description of what is happening, the therapist must be alert to a crisis of incompetence. When the patient experiences a painful reality shock, he represses the awareness of the real failure and displaces attention to the old and well-known defensive melodrama to minimize displeasure when he cannot achieve pleasure.

The narcissistic escape is reinforced when the wife acts as a "melomasochistic" accomplice. They both believe that the consultation should be for improving the couple relationship and fail to recognize the underlying problem of incompetence. This melodramatic "manifest" reason for the consultation masks the dramatic "latent" reason. If this definition is accepted by the therapist, and if he or she treats the sadistic husband as a masochist and treats the wife erroneously as the sadist, the defensive melodrama will be perpetuated. The problem takes on an iatrogenic complication as the consultation further reinforces their defense mechanisms, the problems of sadomasochism and incompetence.

Redimensioning the Topical Spaces

This reinterpretation of narcissism as a melodramatic escape led the authors to redefine this dimension of the topology of the psychic spaces. Freud (1915d) originally proposed a tridimensional toplogy consisting of the Conscious, the Preconscious, which is readily made conscious, and the Unconscious, which strongly resists being made conscious. We propose a pentadimensional model (Gear and Liendo 1981) to solve the dramatic failure. It models the transformation of incompetence into a sadomasochistic melodrama, the therapeutic retransformation of the melodrama into meaningful togetherness, and the incompetence into meta-competence.

The pentadimensional topology consists of: the conscious, which contains the representations of the stereotyped melodramatic pattern of interpersonal mistreatment; the superficial Unconscious, containing the correct representation of the stereotyped melodramatic mistreatment (Frantz 1976); a deeper layer of the unconscious, containing the repressed representation of the traumatic incompetence; a limiting and organizing preconscious frame which, in pathological states, is impermeable, melodramatic, and reactive in its organization; the transunconscious—beyond the limits of the framed, organized and meaningful unconscious— which contains the representations of the more or less neutral data that are potentially transformable into meaningful information necessary for the elaboration of the defensive melodrama and for overcoming the pathogenic traumatic incompetence. It is in this transunconscious space that new subjective choices, options, and dreams can be created (Bruner 1973).

The fifth space, the metaconscious—above the previously described spaces—is the "analytic space" (Viderman 1970), a meta-symbolic position of evaluation from which the other four spaces can be perceived in a new perspective. This notion of the metaconscious is derived from the differentiation between the level of the "object language," as it is described by Tarski (1956), and the level of metalanguage, which is referred to as "language as an object." This is the same type of differentiation as that between thinking, and thinking about thinking. (See Fig. 6-2.)

The Narcissist and the Mirrorist

It is useful to recall the myth of Narcissus. Narcissus saw and fell in love with his own reflection in a water mirror, which he believed to be another person. He declared himself, saying, "I love you." The nymph Echo, hidden from his sight and under a spell

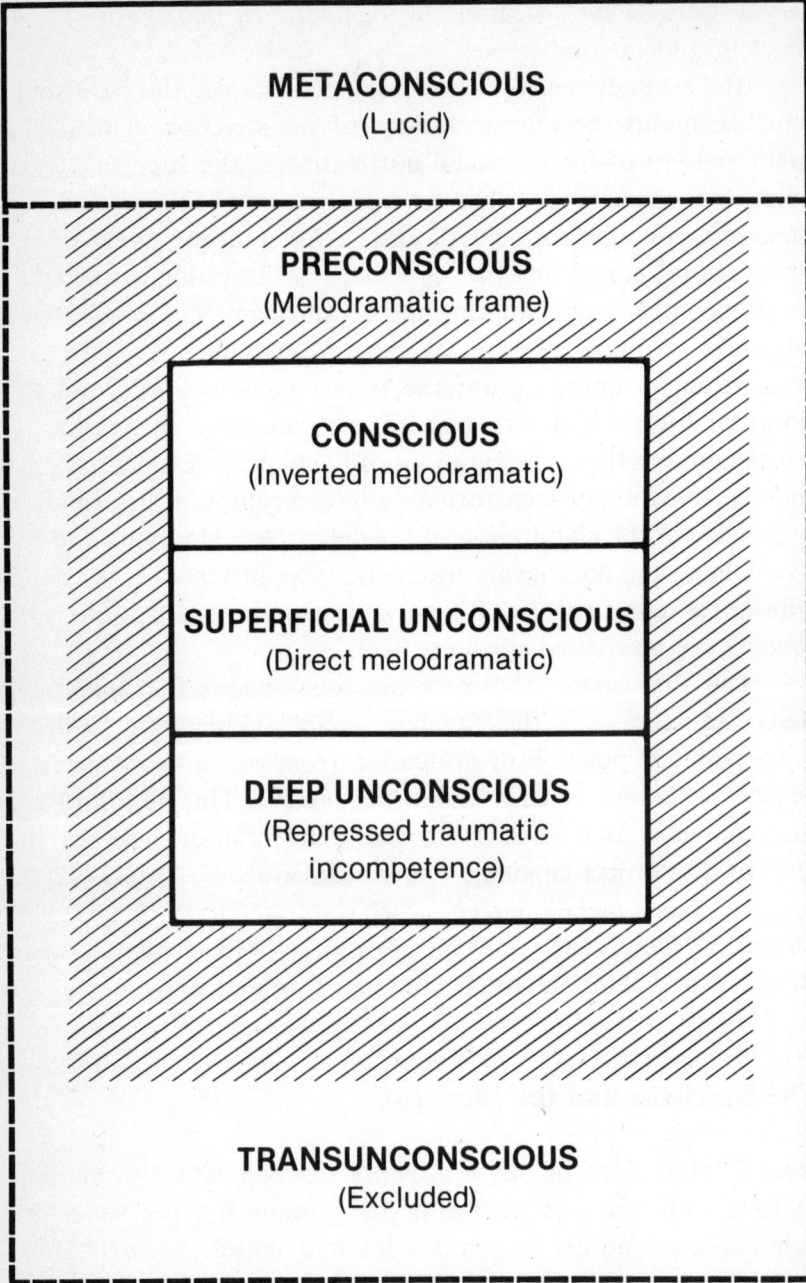

Figure 6-2 The "spaces" of the mind

from the gods, had been condemned to act as an acoustic mirror. She was limited to repeating only what others said. She echoed his words, "I love you." Narcissus was then completely trapped in a visual and auditory double mirroring of himself, as if there were an "other" accompanying him. He attempted to embrace his illusional loved one, and drowned in the mirroring pool.

The melodramatic sadistic self-idealizer and denigrator of others can most easily be identified with the classic concept of a narcissistic personality (Kohut 1977). The masochist is an echoing mirrorist in a self-denigration and idealization of the other. He repeats the closed monologue of the other and perceives himself in the reflection of others. The sadist is like Narcissus in that he imposes his melodrama on others. The masochist is like the nymph Echo, who repeats what others have said and reflects the melodrama of others. The narcissist imposes his personal melodrama on the other, while the mirroristic "echoist" accepts a role in the other's personal script. Both are necessary characters in the personal melodrama generally written by the narcissist. The narcissistic sadist escapes from traumatic incompetence into his own personal melodrama, while the masochistic mirrorist escapes to the melodrama of others, transforming himself into the "other of the other." He is contaminated, and his own weaker melodramatic script is subordinated to that of the other.

The narcissist needs a complementary reflecting and confirming mirrorist. It is not a monadic phenomenon, but rather a dyadic or even a polyadic one. Narcissism and mirrorism are the two sides of the same interpersonal sadomasochistic coin. The melodramatic narcissist is like the sun shining by its own light, whereas the masochist is like the moon seen only by reflected light. The narcissist perceives himself as the center of his own and the other's life.

Freud (1914a) defines the narcissist as someone who believes, "like a beautiful woman," that one was born to be loved but need not give in return—"His Royal Highness." Freud also recognized that there are others who, "like ordinary men," believe that they were born to love others but do not expect to receive. He anticipated the description of the "mirroristic personality" (Gear et al. 1981) complementary to the narcissist. The "loyal subject," the mirrorist, introjects and reflects what the narcissist projects. Together they escape to and maintain the limbo through the shared melodrama. Together, they form a narcissistic couple.

7

Mirrorism, Exhibitionism, and Telemelodrama

PRESSURES OF MODERN society have a strong impact on the possibility of constructing intimate and reasonably stable interpersonal relations (Gear et al. 1983). When there is a lack of strong bonding, nothing impedes minor stress's becoming the reason for changing life partners in the melodramatic or romantic relations.

Transitory and noncommitted relations have become characteristic of our time (Kotlowitz 1987). Contributory factors include the frequent obligation to move from one community to another due to changes in jobs and a more fluid upward and downward social mobility with the daily fight to conserve social status—to "go up" and be "in," or, at least, not to go "down and out."

The projects for transcendence—to go up—compete with those necessary to find intimate togetherness, since even maintaining the status quo makes greater demands on time and resources. Both projects often succumb to the pressures of daily existence.

The Teleaddiction

The arduous recruitment of allies for the dramatic tasks of transcendence, or the finding of melodramatic accomplices for the defensive melodramatic escape, has resulted in the frequent appearance of an even more toxic defense. The telenovel has become the new addiction, of course, more depersonalized and impoverishing than the melodramatic defense.

As it becomes more problematic to establish a stable melodramatic "ghetto," the melodramatic escape to limbo becomes more difficult. Reality shocks, with accompanying pain, cannot be readily defended against. As defenses fall, there is a "return of the repressed." The shared and historically available melodream has become as unreachable as the dream of transcendence. Finding stable company, even for defense, is now a prevalent problem. A remote teleaddiction replaces the "ghetto" and the interpersonal melodrama.

These social pressures, which hinder the possibility of close alliances, are neutralized to some degree by the relationships in the work place. As mass media have become a substitute for intimacy (Richards 1987), technology has further depersonalized and "anti-intimitized" living. The person is more isolated and has the company of "anti-intimate" pastimes. There is no romantic closeness, not even a personalized melodramatic company. Constructive dreams and defensive melodreams require close interpersonal interaction not needed in teleaddiction. The melodramatic script of "soap living" is written by distant others. Passive watching is the requirement. The person is no longer the "subject" of his defense. He has become a "subjected object."

Teledisplacement

The emotional incompetence produces anxiety, psychic distress, and a defensive loss of togetherness. There is a substitution by the pseudotogetherness of melodramatic relations when the social partners exist. Because of the scarcity of partners and allies, the social loneliness is repressed and replaced by the passive mirroristic defensive pseudo "teletogetherness."

The telenovel does not produce romantic or heroic dreams based on real-life drama and is a second defensive escape from awarness of profound loneliness. Its defensive use diminishes intelligence and foments a growing passivity on the part of the audience. The individual becomes disinterested and more alienated from his own life, which becomes more solitary. He has lost both the romantic transcendence in togetherness and the melodramatic dream. "Telecharacters," powerful fictitious personages, become "fictitiously real." They function as "Their Royal Highnesses," the narcissists, while the audience functions more as "their loyal subject," the "telespectator."

To the seven Freudian intrapsychic mechanisms of defense, we here add an eighth. This is the "teledisplacement," based on Melanie Klein's (1955) projective and introjective identification—in this case, "teleidentification." The teledisplacement converts the person into a voyeurist, addicted to the "teleexhibitionism" of the characters of the soap opera. The individual is not in a personal heroic and romantic drama, nor in a personal melodrama with active others. He mirroristically consumes the narcissistic exhibitionistic product of the industry. He lives by way of pseudo-others.

Televoyeurism

Just as the participants of the melodrama are sadists and masochists, the individuals who use the "teledefense" are passive mirroristic voyeurists, who live through the narcissistic characters of the telenovel. The melodramatic sadomasochistic real couple of the personal melodrama is "triangularized" by the introduction of the exhibitionistic teleprotagonists. The telespectators become the voyeuristic others. The characters in the telenovel are "teleexhibitionists." The sadists and the masochists become mirroristic voyeurists. The telespectators identify projectively and introjectively with the telemelodrama's actors.

Freud (1909a) might have interpreted this triangle as a repetition of the "primal scene." The spectator child is limited to look and listen, while the parents, the protagonists, experience sexual enjoyment. The child is excluded. The spectator's oedipal conflicts may be awakened. His envy is attentuated somewhat by the message that the protagonists also suffer to a greater degree than their passive "telespectators." They create the delusion that it is easier and, perhaps, better to be a passive child observer than an active protagonist in a primary scene. It is safer to observe the others in the soap drama as they struggle to be together. The passive voyeuristic attitude has made intimate togetherness an unreachable dream. This teledefense against loneliness and mediocrity compounds the feeling of emptiness and alienation that it produced. The only remaining dream is the voyeuristic one of being in on someone else's contrived togetherness.

Teleidentification

The mechanisms of teledisplacement and teleidentification are illustrated in Woody Allen's film (1985), *The Purple Rose of Cairo*. Here, the spectator wants to escape from a meaningless and hopeless life by entering into the delusion of being a part of a telemelodrama. This lonely woman identifies with the heroine and introjects into her own empty life from the "telepersonages." When she brings her "telehero" to life, although he quickly shows his weaknesses and loses his dazzling charm, she will not—or cannot—abandon the telemelodramatic escape. She is resigned to feeling that there is no intimacy possible in her real life. The telemelodrama supports the inevitability of aloneness. She loses opportunities for togetherness and melodramatic pseudotogetherness and contents herself with an illusionary teletogetherness.

This movie reflects the depersonalizing and "consuming" effect that the exhibitionistic teleprotagonist has on the voyeuristic telespectator. When the hero leaves the screen to enter the viewer's world, he is with her only transitorily. She is again abandoned for the world of the telemelodrama. The young woman is resigned to the passive voyeuristic role of the telespectator. She develops an addiction to a new idealized couple: Fred Astaire and Ginger

Rogers, in the movie *Cheek to Cheek*. For the viewer there can be nothing farther from "cheek to cheek" than the pseudo-"eye-screen" togetherness of a telecontact with these celluloid stars. Astaire and Rogers are those who are cheek to cheek, while the viewer gets only as close as "eye to screen." The glimpses of her own sordid life with an alcoholic man who does not care for her is illustrative of the difficulties that contribute to narcissistic isolation in her couple relationship.

The Soaps

Authors such as Krantz and Robbins write escapist telemelodreams. Robbins (1949) himself labels such authors "merchants of dreams." The reader or audience who has impaired capacity to live in his own personal land, enters the illusionary world of "Krantzland," "Robbinsland," or the "Trumpland" of *I'll Take Manhattan* (Krantz 1986).

Psychiatric consultations today are often of people alone, divorced, and uncommitted. They do not have someone close enough to enter into a melodrama with them. They recur to the escape mechanism of the telenovel, or a drug. They stay in the solitude of an empty apartment. The lost hope for transcendence and togetherness becomes compounded with the pain of isolation and loneliness. They identify with the figures in television series. They see problems similar to their own resolved with an omnipotent facility that increases their sense of ineffectiveness. Telemelodramatism is more grave than melodramatism. The process of teledisplacement leads to an addiction, a "soap opera mania."

The real actors of these teleroles become the focus of an escapist fascination. The public life of the stars becomes the focus of the voyeuristic interest. The stars add to their exhibitionistic roles with biographies and publicity. These reinforce the teleaddiction. From soap opera mania the fan often passes to soap opera living and is interested in the "true story" behind the soap version in publications that specialize in "confidential" exposures. "Kiss and tell" stories are the norm. Envy makes these stars subjects of fascination and targets for attack, even though the viewer often learns that the stars are as emotionally lonely as their fans.

To complete this cycle, the actors involved become victims of this role assumption. They have to continue to live on and off stage as public figures, tyrannized and impoverished by the myths that they helped to create. There are confessions of feeling "terribly alone." Cary Grant once stated, "Everyone would like to be Cary Grant, and so would I." Elvis Presley and Marilyn Monroe fell into drug abuse, in part as a response to the pressure of the expectations of their fans. Actors too are destroyed by their loss of a real identity, trapped in the myth of the characters they portray.

The television or the novel are not the problem. When used to transmit positive heroic romantic themes, they can become stimuli for reality-based personal dreams and inspirations. However, the melodramatized novel, especially the "telenovel," is depersonalizing and creates passive fantasies. It impoverishes and distorts the internal representations of dreams. This alienating "tele-pseudo-togetherness" has a pathogenic effect that works to oppose the therapeutic effect that a true symbolic togetherness will produce.

The teletogetherness with Verdi, upon listening to his operas, or with Picasso, when viewing his art, or with Einstein, when studying his theories, is a productive and an active togetherness. The problem does not arise by the teletransmission of a humanizing culture, but by the teletransmission of a dehumanizing anticulture. When what is teletransmitted is ennobling of man, then it contributes to the transcendence and togetherness of the individual who shares that humanizing experience.

8

Pushers and Users
of the Telemelodrama

THE BEST SELLER *I'll Take Manhattan* (Krantz 1986) will be analyzed here as the prototype of the telemelodrama, through which the teleaddict escapes to and becomes entrapped in the unreachable dreams. The characters in the series are the superpeople who achieve fantastic goals of love and fame with little effort. They live highly emotional melodramatic moments of pathos and sentimentality. Telemelodrama is produced for the demoralized and the lonely.

Even the title implies that the unreachable can be attained easily and that it is possible to dominate New York. We will quote Martha Bayles's (1987) article "Crass Krantz Recrudesces," which is an analysis of the television drama based on Judith Krantz's novel and offer a meta-analysis of her discussion and the argument of the book.

Bayles mirrors and ridicules the telemelodrama. Krantz unconsciously and sometimes cynically defends the ordinariness of ordinary people, yet projects her cynicism onto the vicious media. The others are the "pushers," who idealize the heroes and increase desperation by creating envy and voyeurism. Krantz achieves an inversion of the identities, denouncing through her character Maxi those "other" exploiting sadistic envy-producers, while she plays the individual who lives humbly in Trump Tower.

Bayles demonstrates the alienating escapist "telerelation" of the exhibitionistic superprotagonists and the voyeuristic teleconsumers through the defense of teledisplacement.

Stroll into the high-glitz atrium of Manhattan's Trump Tower, and what do you see? I mean, what is there to look at besides the crowds; the ground-floor forest; the miles of gleaming brass; the six storys of peach-colored Italian marble cascading with water; the acres of immaculate windows displaying emerald-cut diamonds, Louis XV furniture, life-size horses inlaid with Chinese ivory, Swiss champagne truffles and onyx-handled letter openers?

Yes, and there's always yourself. In the glass, in the brass, in the polished marble, even in the water, Trump Tower swims with reflections. Woe to you if you're not ultra-spiffed and ultra-coiffed; you'll regret it at every turn. And conversely, whatever pleasure you take in your own appearance will multiply as you see it mixing and blending with such lavish surroundings.

Judith Krantz works the same way. Her best-selling novels overwhelm us with glittering details of wealth and power; yet they also reassure us with reflected images of ordinariness. Take Maxi Amberville, the heroine of "I'll Take Manhattan." Maxi is the daughter of Zachary Amberville, a mighty magazine mogul who has just died in a freak accident. An envious, unscrupulous and womanizing uncle named Cutter wants to dismember and sell his late brother's empire, so Maxi rushes home from Europe to fight the good fight. Naturally, the poor dear needs a place to sleep, so she buys a $6 million apartment in the stratospheric reaches of (you guessed it) Trump Tower.

Fear not, ordinary mortal. You will be provided with glimpses of somebody's swanky penthouse, probably in Toronto, where most of the interiors were shot. But don't think too hard about these images of opulence being acquired in Canada because even the Krantzes must stick to a budget, and you'll float right up there, without feeling cheated that those 68 floors do not really rise above 56th Street and Fifth Avenue. You'll feel right at home with Maxi as she thrashes around on the Savonnerie carpet shrieking with indignation at the fact that womens' magazines present images of beauty and luxury out of the reach of ordinary mortals.

At first glance it seems ironic that a character from Krantzland should fulminate against the marketing of images that are "too perfect." "These magazines are not selling dreams," wails Maxi, "they're selling put-downs . . . heartache . . . dissatisfaction . . . envy . . . Why can't they sell a magazine that likes women just the way they are?" Needless to say, this outrage would be more convincing if Krantzland ever contained any contented or fulfilled females who did not also happen to be pulverizingly beautiful. (The one ordinary-looking woman in "I'll Take Manhattan" is unloved, abused, crippled, betrayed, and eventually permitted to jump off a tall building of far less architectural distinction than Trump Tower.)

Yet Ms. Krantz is a sly one. Her characters may be gorgeous and filthy rich, but when they're shown achieving success or making their way in the world, it's obvious that they're just folks. Zachary, the good guy, is without social pretension, and so is Cutter, the bad guy. Maxi's mother, Lily, is a bit snooty on account of being an English artistocrat, but her children don't inherit the trait.

Maxi in particular is so down to earth that when we see her squealing with delight in the Trump Tower atrium, we could be in any shopping mall anywhere in America. Nor does Maxi intimidate us with special skills, talent or education. After spending one summer sharpening pencils for her father's art director, and the rest of her life gambling, marrying, and hot-air ballooning, Maxi is able to revamp one of her father's smaller magazines into a new, "woman-liking" format. She does this by thrashing and shrieking, and by manipulating her handsome ex-husband (the art director) into doing all the creative work.

Naturally, Maxi triumphs. Not only does she save the

Amberville empire, she also sells more first issues than any magazine in history except *Life*. Like so many other denizens of Krantzland, she charms the average viewer by being guileless, self-depreciating and inept, while all around her competent, high-powered people exclaim that she is amazing, phenomenal, incredible. No wonder these fantasies work; they invite the public to gaze upon the glossy surface of success, and see there the comforting face of mediocrity.[1]

In the novel Krantz portrays the relationship between the narcissistic sadists and the mirroristic masochists in their complementary roles in the struggle between the bad and the good. The problems of everyday competence to solve real-life problems is not mentioned by the characters. Problems tend to be ignored or are easily solved.

The Impossible Dream

The unreachableness of the telemelodream can be especially appreciated in Bayles's description of the reflections of the "high-glitz atrium of Trump Tower."

This is the superworld of the teleprotagonists. The telespectator's participation is illusory. This is not his real-life situation, and he feels envy, in contrast to felt mediocrity. His role is that of a fascinated voyeurist. The exaggerated narcissism and exhibitionism of the "myth pushers" makes this the perfect scene to highlight the commonplace aspects of the viewer who peeks at this beautiful world. It increases anomie, the sense of the absolute insignificance of self.

Bayles's description includes glittering details. She reassures the reader with sincere reflections. Her style is ironic; it is a healthy protest of the "minority" who are witnesses to the

---

[1] Reprinted with permission of *The Wall St. Journal,* Feb. 23, 1987 © 1988 Dow Jones and Co., Inc.

destructive pushing of the impossible dream. There is hope that the world is not lost to the defensive splitting into the exhibitionistic narcissistic protagonists of the soap-living and the voyeuristic masochist spectators who reflect this soap-living.

There is also splitting between the good and the bad in these plays. The exaggerated sadistic narcissists claim that they are victims. The masochists, in turn, denigrate themselves and idealize the sadist, who becomes confused with the hero rather than the villain. Problems are readily resolved by a "higher power" with little effort. The "good" sadists get their reward, and the bad masochists their comeuppance. The message is that justice will prevail without personal effort. The "good" narcissistic sadists will overcome if one can only wait for the last chapter or final scene.

Being in on the Real Story

These comments of Bayles are given "in confidence," because they tend to represent both the mythical reality unachievable by the teleprotagonists, and the misery and limitations behind the compulsive and alienating exhibitionism. The reader receives a tidbit just as the telespectator is "confidentially" taken into the intimate details of the rich and powerful life of the inhabitants of Trump Tower. If you have no hope of making it to this world, better to be an envious spectator finding fault or an idealizing dreamer identifying with these heroes. Anything is better than being your ordinary unsuccessful real self, excluded from the mythical world of the superpeople. The introjection of the success of the telecharacters and the projection of one's own miserable failure is reinforced by knowing the "real story" about the supercharacters in their super world.

The Paradoxical Protest

Krantz's use of projective identification is referred to as she "pseudo-protests" the use of the media in the exact form with which she has made herself famous as an author. She protests the sale of the impossible dreams while selling them. This truth about falseness is falsely denounced. Ordinary mortals are caught in a paradox. If they identify with the heroine Maxi, they are protesting the bad use of the media to frustrate them and fill them with envy. But they are also identifying with an "ordinary mortal" who lives in a $6 million home. To win they must denounce this paradoxical game. And to be lucid is to be aware of the pain of their situation. They are trapped.

Freud would call such a dilemma the repressive lifting of repression. It contains the essence of the destructive narcissistic-voyeuristic relationship that Krantz denounces, while promoting the teleidentification with the unreachable dream and the uncommon heroine.

Bayles points out the extent of the irony. The ordinary person of the telenovel suffers abuse, depression, and loneliness. The ordinary people who are the telespectators, however, simply project into her their own condition, while introjecting the protest of the heroine.

Somehow this deeply repressed pain of the recognition of personal hopelessness and depression must be identified teleprojectively in the other, to defensively teleintroject an identification with the "Maxis" of the telemelodramatic defense.

Success is easy. We are not threatened by any special effort on the part of these superpeople. They simply accomplish the impossible and everything turns out all right. Talent, study, hard work are not mentioned. Any one of us could succeed. The emphasis of the telemelodrama is on the emotions—the indignation, the envy, and the love and hate of which we are all capable.Emphasis is on the narcissistic "teleprincess," accepted and loved acritically by the "loyal subjects," the mirroristic "teleconsumers." The teleprotagonists, the teleproducers, and the televiewers are all trapped in this unreal world.

The Sadistic Heroine

The melodramatic interpersonal manipulations of a sadomasochistic sort are the "intimate" interpersonal interactions of the telemelodrama. Maxi achieves her goals by sadistic emotional outbursts and by sadistic manipulation of her husband. That is, the exhibitionistic superprotagonist, although an apparently good masochistic victim of the bad plotting uncle is, in fact, an exploiting, dishonest, manipulative sadistic victimizer of her ex-husband.

Like so many other denizens of Krantzland, she charms the average viewer by being guileless, self-deprecating and inept, while all around her competent high-powered people exclaim that she is amazing, phenomenal, incredible.

No wonder these fantasies work; they invite the public to gaze upon the glossy surface of success, and see there the comforting face of mediocrity.

Krantz, the superwriter and defender of the good, real, and simple life, makes, through her heroine, a cynical triumph. She knows what the televoyeuristic public really wants. She is an excellent pusher of unachievable addicting telemelodreams.

9

The "Not Enough Syndrome" and Drug Addiction

THE "NOT ENOUGH SYNDROME" could be explained by the alienating dynamic between the exhibitionistic superbowl stars and their voyeuristic accomplices, the telespectators, from whom they steal the limelight. The common element between this dynamic and the telemelodrama is the unreachableness of the dream. Although it looks achievable, the resources available are not enough. This is not a passive envy but an envious and voracious competition between them. The object is not happiness through fulfilling a transcendent dream in togetherness, but an escape from unhappiness into a utopian galaxy of superstars and infra-satellites. The name of the game is power not for personal realization, but power for itself—power to create envy in the "one-up"-"one-down" game without end or real winners. The "victory" is the power relative to that of another. The payoff is that the other swallows his envy and loses the more brilliant exhibitionistic role. He must accept the humiliation of being cast as a second-string player.

The scandal of Martin Siegel on Wall Street is illustrative. A successful money manager and a respected member of his profession, he is alleged to have committed a crime. It appears that he dedicated himself to inside trading, the illegal trafficking of inside information. Did he take this risk because he was seeking money that he did not "need" and could not use?

The Envious Voyeurist

An alternative explanation is that Siegel had functioned as a successful exhibitionist, a rich "star" who was suddenly outshone and fell into the shadow of an even greater "star" in a larger galaxy. He became an infra-satellite of Ivan Boesky, who took the more brilliant role. This "superstar" of narcissistic exhibitionistic living forced Siegel into an insignificant role as part of the supporting cast. He was in the unfamiliar position of the envious mirrorist. His Gatsby estate could not be compared with the $33 million estate of Boesky. Being placed, as he was, in the role reserved for the other in his melodramatic game is one of the most uncomfortable of experiences. The sadist does not enjoy being forced by an even more powerful sadist to take the role of the inferior, masochistic, devalued "fool." The superstar of the Superbowl detests being an envious loser, outshone and in the shadows.

Although it may have appeared that Siegel sought and achieved a transcendence in togetherness, he seems to have still been in the competitive and alienating sadomasochistic exhibitionistic game of who is superior and who inferior, or in the unending and interminable superpower game of one-upsmanship. The intelligent achievement of a productive and happiness-making cooperative game, based on a certain trust between him and his clients, had apparently been only an illusion. The real game being played was telemelodramatic; how the superstar could evacuate his unhappiness and envy onto the other, forcing him into the lesser voyeuristic role of a powerless loser.

In 1985 Martin Siegel legally earned $1.7 million. In the past few months he was able to scrounge up $9 million as part of his deal with the government prosecutors. At 38 years old he had a Connecticut estate, a million dollar condominium in Manhattan, a family and a reputation as the best and brightest of the new breed.

Eventually, before his anxiety and conscience got a grip on him, Siegel had taken $700,000 in cash from the godfather of this story, Ivan Boesky.

Why did he do it? Why does anyone who is already rich

risk it all for a bit more? These questions will be asked again before the story is over. The public curiosity about the lives of the rich pales before our curiosity about the crimes of the rich.

Words like handsome, self-confident, creative, are attached to Siegel's name. So are words like compulsive and insecure. He dipped into his suitcase for cash spending money to avoid dipping into his capital. He apparently rationalized it by calling the payoff his "consulting fee." Information was the admission card to play the game with the big boys. It was too seductive for him and, finally, for others to hold the admission card and not play.

For some people, the sense of need always stays ahead of their balance sheet. There is no "enough." People begin comparing themselves with the Joneses but may end up comparing themselves with the Trumps. The new breed of deal makers, a friend tells me, operates with the morals of the limo crowd. Siegel went one better: he commuted by helicopter above the crowd. [Goodman 1987]

From the perspective of this analytic model, Siegel's downfall was based on an inability to get into the game of happiness. He was playing an alienating, voyeuristic, envious, melodramatic game of still envious superstars. Previously he had been able to easily win admiration. He himself stopped feeling that he shone, reflecting envy as he got close to the more brilliant superstar, Boesky.

The Tyranny of the Ego Ideal

We will hypothesize about Siegel's dynamics from the available data. Siegel compared himself "unfavorably with the Trumps" rather than with his personal image of his own transcendence in togetherness. In Freudian terms, he was no longer motivated by his Ideal of the Ego, his personal daydream of what he could realize with work and love. He succumbed to the pressure of the ego ideal, that insatiably demanding myth of an unachievable power and perfection. It would appear that Siegel went the way of one of the characters in Gary Trudeau's "Doonesbury," as his colleagues commented:

> He is completely desperate and trading frenzily because he only lacks three hours to be thirty years old and hasn't yet earned his first million dollars.

There are others, however, who could be taken as symbolic of going "beyond" the crowd rather than struggling to be "above" everyone else. They are represented as in the happiness game, not competing to shine brighter, but actually doing so. They reach a meaningful transcendence and, although they may be chosen to represent the unreachable mythical model for voyeuristic telemelodramatic others, they do not need this role to evacuate envy. They have left the envy and insatiable hunger for power behind. The goal for them is happiness through transcendent togetherness. They have not allowed themselves to be trapped in the "role assumption" of the compulsive teleexhibitionist. Nor do they have the compulsive exhibitionistic syndrome of the newly rich. The exhibitionist "one-upsman" superstar does not live better and, inadvertently, show it; he shows off and incidentally "lives worse," since he is really living a more pressured and exhibitionistic life.

Playing a Bad Game Better

Siegel apparently had neither overcome nor left the game of envy. He simply played a bad game better. His incompetence seems to have been in the capacity to enjoy his potential for happiness and to realize himself, comparing himself with his own ideal. He fell into the counterproductive temptation of trying to "fix" the Superbowl game. He sought power and money to be able to evacuate the envy that Boesky's greater exhibition had made him reintroject. He tried to be an inside financial trader because he was an "outside" emotional trader. He was not happy but was escaping from unhappiness, in spite of what many would consider favorable conditions.

The giants also suffer pressures and succumb to drugs. Wall Street brokers, managers, and traders show the pressure and have been reported to use cocaine to keep up with the impossible demands of their idealized roles. They are expected to be consistent and successful forecasters in the unpredictable world of the economy. They must orient their passive, demanding, and dependent mirroristic clients who have the unrealistic expectation of always making gains, even when conditions are unfavorable. If not, they will be abandoned by the disillusioned "faithful," who will now denigrate them, and go to mirror the success of others. Remote possibilities must be magically turned into not only probabilities, but concrete, demonstrable, immediate gains in spite of unfavorable circumstances. (See Figure 9-1.)

The demands of this impossible telemelodrama reduce the physiological endorphines of the active traders, in a dreamed-for and illusory instant supersuccess. In these exhibitionistic protagonists, there is a depletion from exhaustion of the supply. Reality becomes less gratifying because of the incessant demands of the role. Drive for romaticism diminishes, and there is little time or energy to play even the interpersonal melodrama. The person will go to the artificial creation of pleasures, or at least the reduction of anxiety and pain. He may fall into the temptation of abusing artificial "morphines" — the melodrugs: alcohol, marijuana, heroin, and cocaine. Cocaine is not a tranquilizer. It is a direct stimulator of the pleasure center, as is a real success in the personal project. Initially at least, artificial happiness, although momentary, is felt.

The Downward Spiral

The melodrugs transform an illusional defensive melodrama into a delusional telemelodrama and, eventually, into an hallucinatory one. The drug abuser breaks the vicarious melodramatic attachments with reality and with others, lives in an infantile state of wishful thinking. This produces a dangerous illusion of "impunity," an unhappiness- and reality-proof shell. He tries desperately to transform an objective impotence into a subjective omnipotence. There is a progressive reduction in actual options and an increase in utopic choices. The impoverishment of the melodreams is added to the impoverishing melodrugs. This leads to a progressive and inevitable involution in intellectual, emotional, physical, and social competence. The addict is transformed. In some cases, he ends up with only his paleomind, paleoperformance, and paleoenvironment. The paleomind replaces the melomind. This means acceptance only in a paleoenvironment and an even more desperate need to use drugs.

This situation produced by the progressive and, to some degree, permanent reduction of physiological endorphines is a terminal illness. It slowly deteriorates the personality. The person must be somehow restored to a functional level in human relations and socioeconomic achievement. He, like the sufferer from AIDS, has produced irreversible damage in the "immune system"—in this case, his system for handling frustration and anxiety and facing adversity, all necessary in a real search for happiness.

All dreams, according to Freud (1900), are dreams of desire fulfillment. All "morphines" are looked to to satisfy a need to escape from frustration. The healthy id is sustained by physiological stimulation of the endorphines, while the needs of the addict are sustained only by the ingestion of artificial "morphines" and are directed at the escape from unhappiness. Life becomes increasingly remote, as does the possibility of producing real happiness.

Figure 9-1 synthesizes the successive or simultaneous pathogenic options. The defensive melodramatic escape increases the

The "Not Enough Syndrome" and Drug Addiction

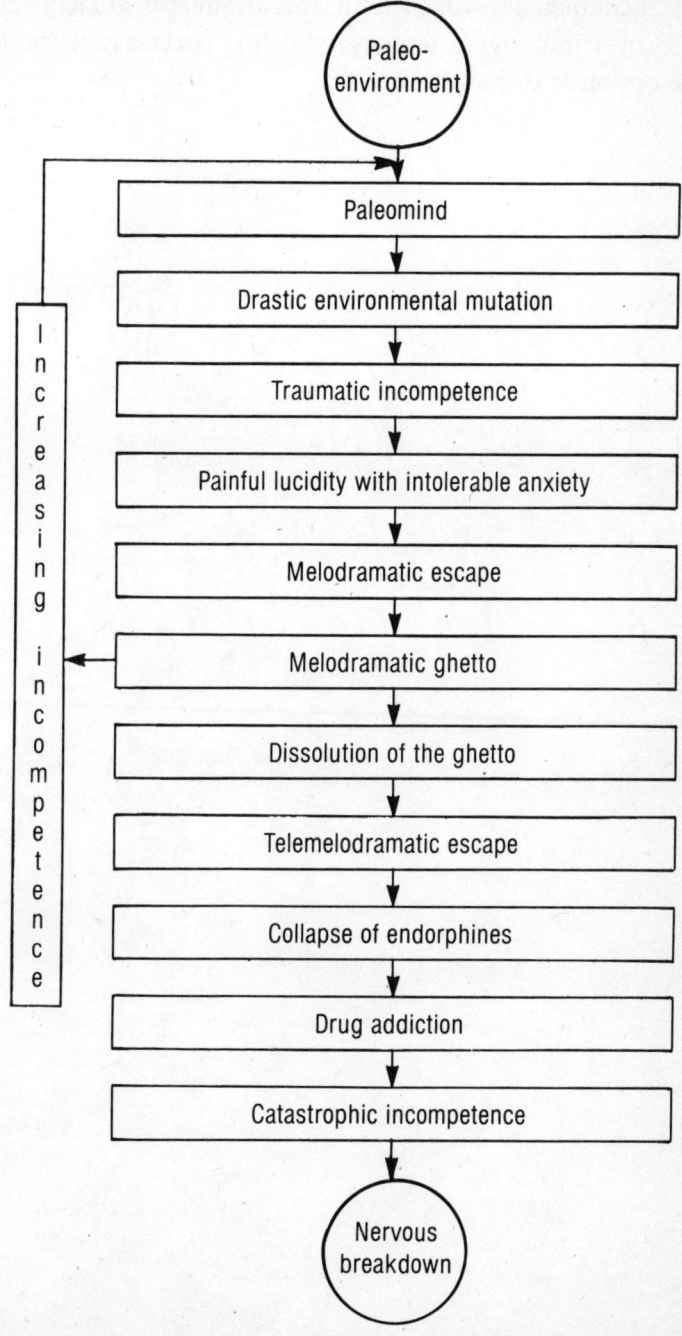

Figure 9-1 Pathogenic options

affect incompetence to contain the traumatic anxiety and to transform it into signal anxiety, which is necessary if the therapeutic option is to be a choice.

Part III

NEW OPTIONS

10

Gaining Competence to Deal with One's Incompetence

10

Gaining Competence
to Deal with
One's Incompetence

PSYCHOTHERAPY IS AN enterprise in which one objective is the recovery or the acquisition of emotional competence. This is essential to the capacity to identify and solve problems relevant to the conception, enrichment and fulfillment of dreams of transcendence in togetherness. This ability to attain happiness for self and others even under unfavorable conditions is dependent, finally, on having the emotional strengths to confront rather than escape from anxieties.

Mental illness results from a deficit in strategic and operational planning. The means available are inadequate to reach the ends. This lack of correlation between subjective choices and objective options makes the dreams unreachable. The therapeutic process is centered on the redesigning and enhancement of choices and options. Both what the person dreams for and his plans to get there must be considered. The new possibilities to identify reachable dreams and implement viable personal projects are the result of a successful confrontation of general and specific problems and how these are solved. Treatment is directed at intellectual, emotional, instrumental, and social enrichment. The mind, the performance, the environment, and even the body must be considered.

The Upward Spiral to Health and Happiness

Therapy proposes to transform an incompetent melomind, derived from the paleomind, into a competent neomind operating in a constructive neoenvironment. The depleted physiological endorphines are restored. This is in response to the optimism and significant pleasures of having achievable goals and being successful in the progressive stages of the personal project. The artificial "morphines" can then be abandoned. For the patient to successfully negotiate his dreams with his reality, he must overcome "sclerophrenia"—a rigid closed-mindedness—and modify the "scleroenvironment" to become competent and to master rather than to cope reactively. This allows the patient to produce happiness and to fulfill dreams in togetherness.

Probably the most crucial therapeutic work is in obtaining the "motivational switch" from a defensive distribution of unhappiness to a productive pursuit of happiness. This is a strategic change in the patient's purpose. He leaves the compulsive defensive "necessity" to escape an unavoidable self-produced unhappiness, and enters into the rational and meaningful desire to reach happiness. The anxiety, depression, and psychic suffering are overcome. The incompetence to fulfill dreams makes for defensive behavior. When dreams are made reachable, behavior becomes productive of happiness. There is a return of hope and energy. The castration complex and the castration anxiety are overcome as strategic planning is improved—that is, as goals and means are effectively negotiated. The patient becomes clearer as to the goals and the means available or potentially available. As the probability of achieving the desired becomes a certainty, the patient confronts and deals resolutively with the difficulties encountered. Signal anxiety helps to identify the problem. There is no traumatic anxiety to paralyze resolutive effort or to push the individual into defense. He can generate or take advantage of the potential in the new relationship that he establishes with the changed environment.

Resolving the Defensive Addiction

We approach the cure of mental illness as we would an addiction. All patients are viewed as addicted to a melodramatic escape from the traumatic pain that results from the perception of incompetence to reach dreams. They have escaped into limbo through the melodrama, the telemelodrama and, at times, the "morphines." They, like the sufferer with chronic physical pain, risk becoming permanently addicted to the "defensive" pain relievers. The addiction is to the melodrama with the sadomasochistic accomplices or the telemelodrama of the exhibitionistic voyeuristic accomplices, with or without melodrugs. The patient has a "melodrama mania," enacted defensively. He lives in a defensive ghetto that supports his parareality.

Therapy must be directed at gradually "detoxifying" the patient. If a drastic withdrawal is attempted, and the subject is forced to leave the melodrama "cold turkey," an "abstinence syndrome"—the psychological "delerium tremens"—may develop. The drug must be reduced gradually and replaced by an attitude of positive resolution. This stimulates the natural endorphines and reduces the need for the exogenous "morphines," whether these be psychological, social, or biological. The patient must replace defensive melodreams for true dreams before he can lose his dependence on the defense. In this way, the abstinence syndrome is avoided. There will be recurrences and small doses of the melodream and melodrama until the patient has reconstructed a neomind in a neoenvironment. The neoperformance brings hope, commitment, and a natural stimulation to the endorphines, which increases energy for commitment to dream fulfillment. The upward spiral has begun.

There is a resistant "sclerophrenia"—rigidity and closure of the mind—which predisposes to defense. The neomind that has become more flexible then becomes capable of analyzing, reframing, and enriching dreams—the strategic goals—of designing viable projects and of a higher level of performance. This determines an enthusiastic commitment to the personal project instead of a compulsive addiction to a depersonalized one.

Therapeutic Competence

From the beginning and throughout the therapeutic process the therapist works to restore and develop the patient's strengths.

It is not enough to limit the therapeutic work to intellectual insight. The patient must reach "experiential insight" reinforced by the therapist and by the environment. The patient must have his anxiety metabolized by the therapist and returned to him in a manageable form. Therapists function as models of emotional competence. The strategy is to identify and confront rationally the emotions produced by the situation. Through their own training analyses, therapists learn and experience the metacompetence to analyze and solve the problem of how they are trying to solve the problem. Analysts must have a capacity to contain and transform their own traumatic anxieties, converting them into signal anxiety, if they are to adequately manage the therapeutic work, avoiding emotional under- or overreactions. When they fail in this, they must know how to recognize and rectify the therapeutic errors, whether they be strategic or operational. The therapist avoids the iatrogenic attitude of "Do as I say, not as I do."

The patient and his environment must "learn" from, with, and through the therapist. They learn experientially to develop the emotional competence to confront relevant problems in the search for happiness (Bruner1973). The therapist functions to transform and to meta-transform the traumatic anxiety that results in the patient's counterproductive escape. This makes possible the resolutive transformation of the patient and his environment. It is vital, therefore, that the therapist possess emotional competence and metacompetence to first solve his or her own incompetences. This is what Bion (1962) would call "to possess an alpha function" or the "capacity of reverie." This significant capacity to metasymbolize is important in confronting and transforming the recalcitrant mechanisms of the melodramatic defense that sabotage therapy. The therapist reacts with a persistent, consistent, and dynamic attitude when confronted by adversity. He must possess some capacity for therapeutic leadership, be a guide through emotional turmoil, and know how to overcome major and minor resistances of both patient and environment. To allow the patient to abandon the melodramatic game, he must do this especially in relation to the traumatic anxieties.

The patient and his environment need support to develop the necessary strengths to overcome the tendency to escape into the repetition compulsion. The patient, even when conscious of the negative effects of his defense, tends to repeat it. The therapist persistently, patiently, and consistently indicates, explains, models, and provides support to maintain the patient. This provides the patient with a model of the tenacity and consistency required to reach a worthwhile goal. The best efforts of the therapist and the maximum use of resources are prerequisites for optimal results. The therapist helps the patient to move toward his desire for transcendence in togetherness.

"Metasolving" Problems

The patient in his environment learns to detect the errors and to correct them systematically, instead of resorting to a quick use of defense. He or she leaves behind the role of melodramatic troublemaker and takes on the role of dramatic troubleshooter. On overcoming the repetition compulsion, he learns to problem-solve and to metasolve the problem of how to address problems.

The therapist must remain as metaconscious as possible about the structure and function of his own conscious, unconscious, preconscious, and transunconscious. This is needed to readily detect the melodramatic transference with which the patient incites him to play the interpersonal defensive game, by inducing in him the complementary role. The therapist must be aware of his own personal melodramatic script or defense which he may countertransferentially and iatrogenically induce in the patient. This can become an impediment to treatment and is most likely to occur when he feels that he is incompetent in his role, without the methods, or unclear about the tasks that must be addressed. The therapist will be escaping from his own traumatic awareness of a therapeutic incompetence.

The therapist's persistence on the right track is essential. All therapeutic processes must overcome moments of crisis. Therapeutic change does not immediately follow insight.

11

Reframing and Enriching Dreams

THE POLITICAL OBJECTIVES of life are those of survival, defensive avoidance, and transcendence in this order. The individual tries first to guarantee his survival. The survival of his sense of self may be more valued than his continued physical existence. Romantic stories are based on the importance of not giving up survival of the essence of self in spite of the threat to the physical self or the social position. Above all else are personal integrity, purpose, love, the "principles," the reachable dream of transcendence in togetherness.

Survival, Defensive Escape, and Self-Realization

In a society of pressures to achieve and of pressures on the intimate relations of family and friends, we are seeing the issue of survival, not self-realization, become the main concern of many. This is reflected even in children's dolls and toys.

Defensive Escape

Those who have achieved some connectedness can enjoy the "luxury" of an interpersonal sadomasochistic defense. They are the blamers and devaluers who play "Which of us is 'guilty' or 'worthless?' " instead of resolving the dramatic problems that they confront in the process of self-realization. They have their melodramatic "ghetto," their "gang" of real people attracted to the same melodramatic game (Glauser 1978). They play an emotional game of unfairness but at least they play it with others. They flee in pairs and gangs from the fear of being unlovable, of "failing" or of being "inferior." In this melodramatic game, there is an unfair distribution of unhappiness. At the same time there is a flight from the anxiety of an incompetence to fulfill the personal dream of transcendence in togetherness. They have tried but with little "success." They are now lost in an interpersonal nightmare or daymare.

Self-Realization

There are those privileged few who are in the "healthy" game of "being," those who have left the problem of survival behind, have met the demands of intimacy. They now try to find their unique expression of what they are or could be.

The task of therapy is determined by the individual's goal stage. A loss of significant togetherness and of personal and realizable dreams is common to the survivors and the defenders. They are the telemelomaniacs, the melodramatists, and the drug abusers. In contrast, the existence of such dreams is characteristic of the transcenders. How to help the survivors and defenders connect with real love and intimacy is a first therapeutic task— that is, how to increase their emotional strengths and contain their traumatic anxiety. A second task is to help them reconnect with a sense of purpose, with commitment and optimism, and to reawaken or to create a personal and reachable transcendent dream. A third task is to help them to convert their transcendent dreams into projects that are viable.

The Impotency Complex

The modern-day castration complex is not what was meant in Freud's time, when a powerful and present father threatened the son if he disobeyed the well-established prohibitions. Today this complex could better be called the "impotency complex," and the father "threatens" because of his own sense of helplessness, the emotional distancing, or the lack of a clear understanding of how to help. The threatening and controlling protector was at least a protector. The threat of the absence of a protector, or even a comforter, affects the capacity for optimism, the sense of personal worth, and the ego strengths to cope with the traumatic anxiety.

A form of corrective "reparenting" must take place to increase emotional strength. The therapist often must take both the "pater" function (Lacan 1966) and the "mater" function (Gear and Liendo 1975). He must model the correction of both the interpersonal and the politico-economic parenting. The "phallus," as defined by Lacan (1966) — as the socializing force which he attributed to father — has been deficient. Or the interpersonal "uterine," "containing," and "love" functions that Gear and Liendo attribute to "mother" — or, more correctly, to the significant other regardless of gender, may require a reinterpretation or a "reframing." When this function is distorted, the individual may be left to a sadomasochistic approach to human relations, but at least there are human relationships. When the function fails completely, the person enters solitude, without the pseudotogetherness of sadomasochism. In "reparenting," it is important that the therapist identify the sphere in which the major problem lies (Gear et al. 1983). The reparenting has to do with developing emotional comptence, a basic ability to cope with the problems of life.

Personal Paradigms and Paradigmatic Psychoanalysis

The "paradigm" (Kuhn 1972) of understanding, the frame which delimits and organizes the person's picture of the world, is not totally conscious or formalized. It is the informal theory with which the person interprets and reacts to the world—his "hidden assumptions." This concept of a "paradigm" allows a greater clarity in this multidisciplinary perspective of psychoanalysis. We have used the word "frame" to emphasize that it forms a boundary. Certain elements or factors are included while others are left out. A frame limits the dimensions of the "mind," selecting and determining what is inside and what is beyond its limits. The frame can also be likened to a prism. It organizes and transforms the enlightening information that passes through it to the intraframe spaces. The conversion has order and predictability. The spectrum is visible, but there is light beyond the spectrum, the "infrared" and "ultraviolet" which, although present, remains undetectable to the ordinary observer. In a parallel way, the preconscious frame organizes the "light of knowledge" in a predictable way. Only that "light" within a certain detectable range can be registered. That which lies beyond the limits of the organizer is not seen. The frame is an organizer that converts information into understanding and fails to integrate other information outside its range.

The psychoanalytic model proposes the description, explanation, prediction, and transformation of the frame of mind with which the patient thinks, feels, and acts; it could be called "paradigmatic psychoanalysis." Therapy should identify the defining and restricting paradigm and how it is organized. It should also consider what is beyond its limits and how this restricts available possibilities.

Psychic Spaces and Therapeutic Goals

Making the preconscious a central and pivotal point of focus led the authors to reconceptualize the psychic spaces. These are discussed in Chapter 6 and are used here in a description of how the lost dream is recovered. The psychic spaces are the inverted intraframe melodramatic conscious; the intraframe directly represented unconscious, with its superficial and deep layers; the constricting preconcious frame; the not necessarily melodramatic transunconscious; and the extraframe metaconscious.

It is from this metaconscious space, on a higher plane of abstraction, that we think about the organization given to our thoughts and emotions. We think about our thinking. This allows us to analyze and transform the incompetent functioning of the intraframe spaces. The task requires a critical metalucidity.

The Freudian topological therapeutic strategy of "making conscious the unconscious" is reformulated from this new five-dimensional topological perspective: "to make metaconscious the conscious, unconscious, preconscious, and transunconscious." The therapeutic objective, in terms of psychic spaces, is to reframe and give a new understanding to experience. The individual derives neodreams which, although new, are emotionally meaningful as well as achievable. As a result, the castration complex and the related traumatic anxiety are overcome.

This is achieved by making the patient metaconscious to his dilemmas and choices in which the either-or dilemma of two extremes is eliminated. From childhood one organizes experience in contrasting categories, such as altruistic-egoistic, good-bad, hot-cold. If the choice is limited to these extremes, one is confronted by a dilemma. To escape from the dilemma, this bipolar reduction must be identified and denounced. This step broadens possibilities. The person can better conceive, plan for, and reach the dreamed-for.

> Edward is a 30-year-old alcoholic who stopped drinking two years ago. He is the only son of a violent alcoholic man and an erratic and aggressive mother. His mother separated from the father when the patient was 10 years old. She threw Edward out of the house when he was 16. Edward claims not to have been able to explain this. He had done nothing out of the ordinary. She did not give reasons but provided money

for him to live in a room at a neighbor's house. The mother was not affectionate; she was not interested in his schooling. At the age of 17 he began to drink.

Edward is not married. His choice of girl friends has always been older women. He says that he does not like to go out, to dance, or to be with young women, whom he considers "superficial." His girl friend of the last six months—Mary—has been married three times. He is fond of her three children. She treats both Edward and her children in an aggressive and arbitrary way. Her mother and father, who are wealthy, and her third ex-husband, financially support her. She does work, being the owner of a boutique given to her by her father, who manufactures clothing. She makes no profit and complains constantly that it is her partner's fault.

Edward is in real estate. He buys, renovates, and sells old houses and apartments. He is economically stable and able to meet his own needs, and he contributes to the expenses of Mary's household when he is there. He has not moved in permanently, maintaining his own apartment. He does, however, spend a great deal of time with her.

His reason for consultation is that he wants to understand his girlfriend. He is afraid that the relationship is going to terminate and wants to do everything possible to save it.

We will illustrate the steps in paradigmatic psychoanalysis, using this case.

Making the Melodramatic Metaconscious

First, the person becomes metaconscious of his melodrama, which is dilemmatic and sadomasochistic and is perceived in an inverted form. The following quotes from a session demonstrate the melodrama and the paradox.

She got mad and threw me out. I had bought steaks for the whole family. She was frying them and I was setting the table. I put the plates and cups for everyone, but I became distracted and I only put a knife and fork for me. She became so mad! She didn't say anything, but took my steak and threw it out to the dog! Then she threw me out with it. I don't understand. The last time when she let me back I bought roses for her and she had another fit! She said that I bought too many and that any man who cared for her would at least know how many vases she has. Oh, and once before she said that she was mad at me because I didn't go into her personal hiding place to get out her documents. I wouldn't go into anyone's private "safe" without their express permission. She said that that was a sign of lack of intimacy and that I was distant and too reserved. Oh, yes, then later she told me that the real reason that she had thrown me out was because I had corrected the children. But I did that nicely! Do you think that I have a problem with closeness? I am afraid of splitting. She says that I don't get out my resentment.

Edward is playing a sadomasochistic game in which he is devalued and blamed masochist, qualified as the inferior one—inconsiderate, lacking in intimacy, valueless as a partner because he is unable to be assertive. His partner is sadistic but qualifies herself as suffering mistreatment and lack of consideration at the hands of Edward.

Edward seeks to have company. He thinks that if he could only understand he could please the other and guarantee that he would not be alone. He submits and seeks to please. The other, however, is only "pleased" when able to express blame and to make him the depository of her negative feelings. This allows her to export her displeasure although not achieving pleasure. He submits to abuse to avoid abandonment, but the result is that he is abusively and continually abandoned or threatened with abandonment. He continues to be confused as to why the other is not "pleased" in spite of his efforts and sacrifices.

The Direct Representation of the Melodrama

Second, the person becomes conscious of the direct representation of this melodrama from the superficial layer of the unconscious. The inverted conscious perception is corrected.

> The therapist pointed out that in the relation between them Mary repeatedly devalued him and blamed him for the difficulties in the relationship. Consciously, he tended to accept this but as he analyzed the behavior in his therapeutic sessions, it was apparent that she was not in a relation of "confidence," since she had not said what she felt about his correcting her children. She was impulsive and abusive. She did not ask why he had not put cutlery for everyone. She simply humiliated him. She did not consider the feelings of the children, who seem to love Edward and who showed distress at being deprived of him for an arbitrary number of days until she wanted him back.
>
> It was suggested to Edward that when Mary confused him with her accusations and anger, he might discover that what she said was true of him was, in fact, true of her.

Facing the Fear

Third, he must confront the affect — the anxiety — provoked by the traumatic incompetence and related to the certainty of "castration," or the awareness of the unreachableness of the dream. This has been repressed in the deep layer of the unconscious. Emotions can only be realigned as they are identified and as the perception of what is happening is corrected. New experience must be provided in the "corrective parenting." A new emotion of optimism comes with the anticipation of being able to fulfill the dream.

Edward's most important dream seems to have been interpersonal; that of living in a predictable and safe world where he could understand and count on another. His "primary" impotence seems to have been in the area of meaningful relating. His infantile world was lacking in capacity to contain anxiety and to give the frightened child a sense of reason and congruence.

His lack of social skills is very evident in his not knowing how to "play," to have "fun," to sing, to dance, or to approach another person who is able to love as well as be loved. He is also unable to deal with his own angry feelings. He perceives his mother's and his girl friend's irrational anger but does not register his own. He is relatively productive in the economic sphere. He is reliable, honest, and hardworking, has initiative, and treats his employees well. When asked about his dreams and desires, he confesses to want a family and to want to be able to relate without appeasing all the time.

These are Edward's conscious desires. In his unconscious is a great fear of the closeness that he longs for. His early experience has convinced him that people are erratic and unpredictable. His later experiences further confirm his thesis. He does not believe in the possibility of fulfilling his "dream" of being accompanied by a predictable, loving, and comforting other who will be constant and will understand and be understandable. When he gets into an interpersonal situation with others who value him and who do not really want to be appeased, he feels even greater insecurity, because he does not know what to "offer" except a pathological tolerance of abuse. He fears that he will be abandoned and hurt because he offers nothing to the relationship. This makes him withdraw, and he returns to his melodramatic ghetto of erratic, intolerant others. There is a constant return of the repressed fear.

Challenging Frame Constrictions

Fourth, the restricting preconscious frame, which is both the cause and the effect of traumatic incompetence, must be denaturalized, broadened, and made flexible.

The constricting preconscious frame has certain "universal deficits." It is narrow, being constricted in the interpersonal to the sadomasochistic. He can conceive and act only in relations that are appeasing to an incomprehensibly angry other or face the threat of solitude.

The paradigm is oversimplified and bipolar in its organization, the categories receiving their significance principally in relation to the affect "anger" or a complementary "fear." People are either "angry" or "angering." If they are angry, they are frightening and must be appeased. If they are angering, they are frightened and appeasing. The oversimplification and the bipolarity result in a paradox in which there is no way to solve the problem of intimacy. If Edward asserts himself, he is attacked and abandoned for not pleasing the other. If he submits, he is attacked and temporarily abandoned, since he has tacitly accepted the evaluation of the other that he is the unpleasing and worthless member of the pair. He cannot solve the problems of intimacy from the paradigm with which he is reasoning.

He accepts as "natural" the erratic behavior of the other. He does not question the sanity of his mother or his girl friend. He tries to explain the actions of these people as if they were reactions to his behavior and therefore controllable by appeasement or by correcting what he does that the other does not like. When it was pointed out to him that most people would quickly conclude that his girl friend is a very narcissistic person who explodes with him when she is personally ineffective or frustrated, he found it hard to grasp that the focus of looking to himself as the cause of the behavior was not "naturally" the "correct" orientation if he is to develop a more effective "understanding."

Reframing and Enriching Dreams

New Dreams, New Options

Fifth, the Transunconscious extraframe space, from which new data are incorporated, must be examined. What has been represented but incorrectly signified as not pertinent may now be included. These neutral transunconscious data, which have been transformed into significant and helpful information, are incorporated into the expanded intraframe spaces, establishing a more viable relationship between means and ends in the task of producing happiness. The strategic goal and the tactical plan are negotiated with this clearer view of the person's reality, his assets and his options.

In this case, attempts have been made to understand the significant other (mother, father, and girl friend) as if their reactions were comprehensible in terms of the behavior of Edward. He has not examined their behavior as dependent on their own internal conditions rather than as responses to his behavior. The therapist helps the patient to signify as pertinent those failures and frustrations that he knows the other is suffering. For instance, his undisciplined failing partner criticizes him for being on time, calling it a pathological "hangup." The consensus of his friends is that Mary is unpredictable. It is not possible to know if she will show up, and certainly it is predictable that she will leave everyone waiting. As well, he notes that she tends to attack when she has lost money in her business or has had a fight with her partner. The "lucid witnesses" find him a considerate fellow and consider that she is "unpleasable" not because of what he fails to do. She attacks when she needs to get rid of her own personal uncomfortable feelings. His tendency to devalue social skills as "superficial" is reevaluated. He is helped to see that what is "superficial" is the tendency to stay in the sadomasochistic game of blame and devaluation, not such things as dancing or singing.

Although this psychoanalysis begins as a traditional analysis, making conscious the original paleodreams and derived melodreams, it does not stop there. The therapist analyzes with the patient from the metaconscious position, and searches for new extraframe transunconscious nondilemmatic alternatives, so that there is a representation of a reachable intimate dream and togetherness. The reachableness of the desired permits optimism and energy to flow into the void of pessimism and indolence. In this example, the patient must see that his choice of partner and his attempt to appease as a way of guaranteeing company are what make him a captive of an eternal struggle for emotional survival. For Edward, to change or leave the couple relationship was an essential condition for developing intimacy.

New romantic dreams are produced by reframing and building up the historic desire. It is not just the generation of neodreams, unconnected with previous melodreams, but also these neodreams related to intimate past desire. When this patient faced the pathological nature of his couple relationship and developed social skills, he was able to accept that the couple relationship would not endure an assertion of his rights or his worth. He was able to risk attempts at closeness with a woman able to be intimate. His melodream of obtaining company by accepting abuse was converted into a neodream of sharing efforts and criteria for evaluating these efforts as he established a functional family with his new partner. As well, he became active in Alcoholics Anonymous as a sponsor of others who were seeking help. The neodreams did not exclude the paleodreams; they contain them in a transformed or realistically improved form. The constructive analytical process synthesizes and integrates the paleodreams with his reachable neodreams. In this way they conserve their intimate significance. They coincide with the deep characteristics of his identity and sense of self. In other words, in order to be emotionally significant for the patient, the neodreams must always be based upon the historic desire, the old dreams. The difference is that in their new form they can be fulfilled. There are new subjective choices and new objective options. A man such as this will not be comfortable with a neodream of wealth and

Reframing and Enriching Dreams

opulence. He is going to enjoy such things as social service. His new dream, like his old, will be one of somehow understanding and helping another. In the new dream state he will have a new and clearer understanding of what it is to help and what must be understood. He will continue to give but, as well, will make reasonable demands on the other. He will reframe his understanding and will understand his failure to confront as a spoiling and weakening act. He will no longer confuse masochism with helpfulness. His exact personal project will reflect opportunities in the environment. In his case A.A. provided opportunities for service.

The Pleasure Principle and the Reality Principle

For Freud (1938), a fundamental objective of therapy is to replace the pleasure principle with the reality principle. This means the replacement of the defensive "escape principle"—escaping from anxiety—by the realistic "seeking principle"—seeking to produce happiness. The escape principle leads to an immediate anxiety reduction through melodrama. The seeking principle leads to a search for a realistic romantic dream. To exaggerate, we might say that "paradigmatic psychoanalysis" begins precisely where traditional psychoanalysis ends. Traditional psychoanalysis proposes to make the unconscious conscious and to put ego where superego had been. Paradigmatic psychoanalysis goes beyond and above the organizing limits of the conscious and unconscious spaces. It moves toward a lucidly and intelligently critical metaego, above the ego and superego and beyond the already known and signified into the potential information and understanding of the Transunconscious. It is not limited to "re-cognize" the old unreachable dreams or the melodreams. It looks to create new dreams based on old. These are the reachable romantic neodreams. There is an extra frame—metaanalysis and metasynthesis. Edward had to face his fear of the intimacy that he most desired and the impossibility of constantly appeasing and still developing the conditions for intimacy.

From Dogmatic Superego to Sensible Metaego

Upon replacing the melodramatic pleasure principle with a romantic reality principle (Freud 1911), the impulses are consciously transformed and lucidly governed by the individual, instead of by a short-term interest in tension relief. The patient stops the counterproductive escape from his impulses and begins to resolve the dilemmas that impede his search for happiness. To achieve this change in governing principles, a sensible ego must be put where the dogmatic superego reigned. That is, the patient must begin to confront problems flexibly instead of doing so in a rigid and restricting manner, based on an obsolete value system. The superego that was uncritically internalized by the child has been "denaturalized." The neomind is intelligent and has relatively objective critical judgment.

Reframing to enhance the defensive melomind, transforming it into a productive neomind, and doing the same with performance and environment seems to be the most powerful symbolic maneuver in overcoming the false melodramatic dilemma. The melomind puts forth that false choice between hopeless utopian romanticism and the viable illusory or delusional narcissistic melodrama. This latter is reachable and gives immediate relief from depression and anxiety.

Overcoming Psychoaddiction

By adding to options, the pathogenic dilemma is transformed into a resolvable problem. The dilemmatic no-win choice between a depressing realism or a melodramatic illusion is overcome by

Reframing and Enriching Dreams

creating the new choice of romantic realism. This choice, because it is reachable, works like an antidepressant. It produces renewed enthusiasm for happiness. Edward's no-win choice was to submit to an erratic, aggressive other and to be rejected as valueless or to confront this other and to be rejected for the confrontation.

An iatrogenic perpetuation of the patient's dilemma is produced if the therapist remains trapped in and "framed" by the limits of the patient's melodrama. It is imperative to analyze, reframe, and enhance the paradigm itself. Therapeutic work revolves around the fight between the pathogenic and therapeutic frames. The pathogenic frame is preconscious, although it organizes the unconscious and conscious content. The therapeutic frame is metaconscious and is deliberately proposed by the therapist. If the patient manages to reframe the therapist, and not the therapist the patient, treatment is transformed into a chronic and counterproductive "psychoaddiction." This is a frequent occurrence and contributes to diminish the image of psychoanalysis as a powerful therapeutic instrument.

Psychoanalysis, in these circumstances, then is an interminable and counterproductive relationship of emotional dependency. Far from resolving the problems of the patient, it supports the patient's repetition compulsion. For instance, if the therapist simply insists that Edward rebel against this sadistic treatment and that he fight interminably with Mary, the therapy will have managed to reverse the roles in the sadomasochistic game, rather than putting an end to the game. The therapist must also avoid the countertransferential role of imposing a solution arbitrarily. Edward must convince himself in his own time of the sadistic nature of the relationship. The therapist must patiently and consistently point out the events and actions and not impose a solution that seems arbitrary to Edward.

Transunconscious Enrichment

To summarize, the patient resolves his false pathogenic dilemma between an unrealistic romanticism and a real melodramatism.

The patient encounters a reachable realistic romanticism in his transunconscious. He needs to develop his alpha function and make his metaconscious lucid. The patient must correct his inadequate perceptions, thoughts, and feelings and begin to perceive, think, and feel what has been ignored, denied, or not experienced in a significant way before. The patient thus establishes new intellectual, emotional, and instrumental dimensions within a new frame. The most noble of human pleasures is generated in this reflexive metasymbolic space. It is the pleasure which Leonardo da Vinci called "the ecstasy of understanding." Pythagoras called it "the philosophy of the supreme music."

By introducing new inner choices from the transunconscious and new objective options from the transenvironment these dilemmas can be resolved. The dilemma results from what Watzlawick (1974) called "those terrible oversimplifications." It is a false and mutilating reduction of choices that produces a false dilemma. The melodramatic frame constrictions give the patient only two choices, between an unbearable anxiety of realism or the melodramatic defense against this anxiety. There would be, therefore, only two roles in the melodrama: sadistic narcissism or mirroristic masochism. The style of the players and the specific content of the "play" is personal, but the game is stereotyped. There is only the depersonalized exhibitionism or voyeurism of the telemelodrama.

The same understanding of the nature of a limiting paradigm and a false choice allows the patient to overcome other false dilemmas. For example, a hysterical person is often caught between two unsatisfactory options. He knows how to be insincerely seductive or sincere but unpleasing. He has learned to equate pleasantness with seduction and unpleasantness with sincerity. He needs to put these possibilities back together and to be pleasant in a sincere, friendly relationship. The paranoid melodramatic dilemma loses the choice of reality testing and trust. The paranoid perceives his options as distrusting indiscriminately or trusting totally. To discriminate and identify the trustworthy by being alert to reality testing is what must be learned. The melodramatic dilemma of the obsessive results from equating responsibility with a rigid and compulsive approach. Flexibility is confused with irresponsibility. He must learn that these categories are not mutually exclusive.

Identifying Friends and Enemies

To obtain transcendent togetherness, what would have to be reframed, according to strategic game theory, would be the destructive game of the individualist (Steiner 1974). Although it may be disguised as a false altruism, in this competitive game "friends are treated like enemies." There is a "competition" with the allies and an alliance with the "competitors." This apparent inconsistency has an explanation. The masochist and the sadist are in a narcissistic pact. Each plays the same defensive game and accepts the apparently unjust distribution of unnecessary suffering perceived as inevitable. The sadist considers the masochist an enemy but still protects himself from the loss of the relationship. He tries not to permanently destroy the masochist with an excess of sadism. Complementarily, the masochist tries not to overdo the masochism and be definitely destroyed. There is a competition to escape from a certain type of nontraumatic anxiety where the sadist always wins and the masochist always loses. They cooperate because they both need the melodramatic game to escape from the greater anxieties of a failure to deal competently with vital life problems. The disqualified masochist idealizes the disqualifying sadist and takes him as his friend. Both the sadist and the masochist must continue to be "friendly enemies," if they are to continue their much-needed complicity for the melodramatic escape from anxiety. The melodramatic game is a major tranquilizer. The melodramatic role is a minor tranquilizer for the sadist and a minor source of anxiety for the masochist.

The common enemy in the melodrama is the person who tries

to produce or share happiness with them. Such sharing implies eventual exposure to the anxiety that they struggle to avoid. The rule that governs the psychodynamics is: a minor anxiety, a minor defense directed at distributing displeasure, and a minor resistance to a therapeutic intervention; a major traumatic anxiety, a major melodramatic defense, and a major resistence to therapeutic change.

The Therapist as Superego of the Superego

Therapy is meant to help transform the competitive individualist game of the "sum zero type," in which one wins at the other's expense, into a "more than sum zero" game, where a productive partnership enriches both players. The partnership is productive. This therapeutic mutation into the fruitful game of "partnership" is achievable only to the degree that the analytic work manages to reframe and transform the rigid and oversimplified value system that Freud (1912b) termed the superego. It is not derivable from the paleoethical system that produced the "meloethic." This idealizes the masochist but rewards the sadist. The questioning must be from a metaethical plane that perceives, in a nondogmatic way, what is said and what is done, and metaperceives the relationship between sadist and masochist as both a false and an "unintelligent" arrangement that limits real cooperation and fair and productive sharing. The individualist game excludes the possibility of all other games of a happiness-producing sort. They cannot play the game of reciprocal altruism, based on an intelligent and cooperative disposition. A mutually beneficial relationship cannot take place. They are stuck in the defensive game of distributing existent displeasure.

To put this sensible ego where the dogmatic superego had been, Freud (1915b) recommends a second fundamental objective of therapy—"to make conscious the unconscious" by using "in-depth" interpretations that make the patient conscious of his motivational switch. He has stopped seeking happiness because of a need to escape from anxiety. The person is addicted to the seemingly low-cost solution of a melodramatic escape. But like most addictions, it does not solve the problem but rather perpetuates it. This becomes counterproductive and costly in the long run.

The therapist should act as the "superego of the superego." He should be a "judge" who respects the Kantian principle of "You must implies that you can." The purpose is to achieve that the binding and blinding dogmatism of the melodramatic superego be replaced by an intelligent and intelligentizing metaego. The masochistic superego is analyzed in its tendency to give compulsively and not get. This is replaced by an altruistic intelligence that is based on an equilibrium between giving and getting. This implies that the melodramatic paleoethic of the superego be naturalized and removed in its organizing function from the preconscious frame. It is clarified from the position of the lucid critical metaconscious. The therapist promotes an ethic that relates contribution to retribution between the patient and his environment, and which incorporates the concept of intelligent altruism.

Minor and Major Resistances

Only by leaving the restrictions of the melodramatic frame can the game be changed qualitatively. Anything else gives only the new alternative of another variation of the same game. In Kuhn's terminology (1974), therapy seeks a "metatransformation of the paradigm." This is a revolutionary type of change and a break with the limitations of the past. The intellectual, emotional, and instrumental schemes that govern the manner in which the patient understands, feels, and reacts to his environment are to be revolutionized. This implies a qualitative change in the narcissistic mind. It is not enough to limit the sadist to be less sadistic or transform him into a masochist, or the reverse with the masochist. Each must abandon the sadomasochistic game used to escape from major anxieties to minor anxieties. When the major anxieties threaten to recur, there is a crucial therapeutic resistance.

It is a clinical observation that minor resistances occur in the area of bringing the superficial unconscious to consciousness. The therapist uses interpretations so that the sadist can perceive his role of dominating and victimizing. He can be forced to an inversion of roles where he reluctantly assumes the role of masochist. The masochist does the same. Both, however, tend to present a major resistance in changing the preconscious melodramatic frame and leaving this now-conscious but not voluntary sadomasochistic melodrama. Here, change implies confronting traumatic anxieties.

Making metaconscious the unconscious sadomasochism is an important battle to win. To manage to change the sadomasochistic game imposed by the preconscious frame is to win the war. Consequently, from the beginning of therapy there will be a focus on what kind of resolution to give to the sadomasochistic defense. The patient will attempt unconsciously to include the therapist in a melodramatic definition of the relationship. He will select, induce, and reinforce the countertransferential role in his therapist. The therapist will attempt to identify and redefine the pathogenic relationship based on a ruinous individualism into a resolutive relationship based on reciprocal altruism. The therapist will achieve his objective of helping the patient to produce happiness when both have elaborated the melodramatic transference and entrapping, countertransferential, melodramatic reaction. If melodramatic transference and countertransference are not elaborated and overcome, therapy at best will produce only a better playing of a bad game. It will fail to make the change to a better game.

These therapeutic changes take place on the level of the

Reframing and Enriching Dreams

paradigm, performance, and environment and produce a mutually reinforcing stability. Traditionally, analytical therapy used two basic instruments: "in-depth interpretation" and "analytic setting." The structure and content of the intraframe melodramatic conscious and unconscious was interpreted. Curiously, this was done within the limits placed by the existent preconscious melodramatic frame. If interpretations were limited to operating with the intraframe spaces, the analytic setting pragmatically had to question and open the frame. As a result, it permitted an experiential extraframe amplification. The analytic setting, antimelodramatic by definition, redefined pragmatically the sadomasochistic game, although in-depth interpretations were limited only to describing and explaining without transforming it. The paradigmatic psychoanalysis that we propose here attempts to extend and deepen therapeutic mutations barely initiated in the analytic setting. Instruments of this theoretical position include "amplifying interpretations." These are metaconscious openings created in the preconscious frame and metaconscious enrichments coming from the extraframe transunconscious.

The classic intraframe "working through" of the melodramatic conscious and unconscious is completed with the "working out" of the repressed traumatic incompetence. It also breaks through the restrictions of the melodramatic frame. This is accompanied by an "amplification and enrichment" of the intellectual, emotional, and instrumental competence of the patient and his environment.

All "working through," "working out," "breaking through," and "amplification and enrichment" of the incompetent melomind can neither be completed nor sustained without a simultaneous transformation of the incompetent meloenvironment that reinforces and perpetuates the paleoparadigm. It is precisely here that the therapeutic work begins as the patient and his environment begin to work within an antimelodramatic, therapeutic neoenvironment. The therapist must have strategic and technical metacompetence for this work. To recognize and overcome the incompetences that emerge in the course of treatment (Kolb 1984) depends on the exercise of a competent therapeutic leadership to help the situation when the inevitable environmental and individual resistances begin to appear, especially those resistances to change in the preconscious frame and its paradigm.

12

Uncovering the Repressed Story

THE TASK OF recovering mental health is centered, according to Freud (1912), on the struggle to control the transference on the part of the patient and to control the countertransference on the part of the therapist. In therapy, the patient will unconsciously attempt to "transfer" his melodramatic defensive game to the therapeutic situation, even though this is counterproductive. To escape anxiety, the patient attempts to have the therapist participate in the game by accepting the complementary role. The patient will try to play this more comfortable game of the distribution of minor melodramatic anxieties rather than face the overwhelming anxiety of the actual dramatic crisis.

Transference in Therapy

The playing of the game is a psychological tranquilizer and an antidepressant. Since it maintains a familiar congruence to the sense of understanding, it also avoids the psychotic state of chaos. If the therapist unconsciously enters into the game, this impedes him from acting as an intelligent and resolutive ally. The therapist must be dedicated first to understanding, then to the conscious playing, and finally to the changing of the melodramatic game. The patient and his environment tend to resist a changing of the game. They invite the therapist to participate as a blind accomplice in a preconsciously structured game, not as a metalucid ally in the therapeutic work.

From the first phase of treatment, the therapist must be alert to this danger and avoid accepting the patient's maneuvers to melodramatically "frame" him, or both will remain in the melodramatic game in melodramatic roles assigned or induced by the patient. The therapist is trapped "inside" the organization of the frame and will be unable to reframe the narcissistic ghetto or stop the compulsive game.

An Untold Story

The patient and his "environment" seek therapy because they are in a crisis that reflects intellectual, emotional, instrumental, and/or physical incompetence. Not only are they unable to produce happiness, but they are also experiencing an intolerance of their suffering.

When patients come to treatment there is an "untold story." It is unusual for them to refer to the failure and incompetence that underlies the anxiety. On the contrary, the "manifest" reason for the consultation usually refers to a melodramatic interpersonal crisis. They have displaced their attention from the actual problem. They reveal sadomasochistic excesses and seem to suffer a sadomasochistic escalation in their interpersonal behavior. The "latent" unconscious motive is the unrevealed dramatic story. That is, it is related to a traumatic incompetence, a daymare experience, which has impeded happiness in togetherness and leads to a traumatic anxiety with a large dose of inevitable unhappiness.

The Masking Melodrama

The patient does not immediately report his "incompetence complex." He doesn't say that he cannot reach his dreams. Rather, he complains that he is a victim or a victimizer of others. He does not see that he, as Freud (1914b) would say, is provoking what he fears. The feared is provoked in the defensive avoidance of the vital incompetence, which has been repressed and displaced. The sadomasochistic excesses do not seem to be what the patient most fears. What he fears is his inability to use the defense successfully against the major anxiety provoked by his consciousness of a hopeless incompetence.

The melodramatic manifest reason for the consultation tends to replace a repressed latent one. The therapeutic work must "decenter" the patient from his melodramatic monotheme and "recenter" him on the actual dramatic failure to reach dreams because of an incompetence. These underlying problems must be addressed in both the patient and his environment.

The manifest melodrama and the latent dramatic story are illustrated in the following case history.

> John is a 32-year-old department head in his father's company. He complains that his wife is not interested in sex and that she feels that he pays no interest to her or her needs. He notes that she talks on the phone to other men. She has asked him for a divorce. He becomes depressed and feels worthless. He suspects an affair.
>
> He is the only son of an intellectual father, who felt obliged to show his own father that he could also do business. The father tends to devalue. He considers John to be ineffective and spoiled. The father has not given John a contract or a job description. The father has not registered the company. The mother is a depressive who has had treatment in the past. She is not given much attention or importance by the father. One sister is schizophrenic and another is alcoholic.
>
> The wife is the only child of a successful immigrant who has become a millionaire as a result of his capacity to perceive opportunities and to take advantage of them with hard work. She was told by her father that she is a special and talented woman who deserves the best. She is accustomed to having what she wants. Her father gave her a diamond

necklace for Christmas; her husband gave her a new dress that she felt was out of style. The wife studied literature at the university but did not graduate and has never worked. She does not want to come to therapy, since it is her husband that she perceives as problematic. She has a history of having left college at exam time because of anxiety and phobia. She married shortly after. She was in treatment only until her symptoms improved, at which time she said that she didn't need any more help and that she was perfectly fine.

John is a college graduate. He has worked in other companies, generally for relatives or family friends. He leaves jobs after about a year, feeling that he is not progressing. When he left the last job, his wife threatened divorce. He tells of her demands that he go to the store for her, that he stay up all night if the baby is sick. He complains that she wants him to go out to parties three or four times a week. He tends to "disappear" to a friend's or his parents' house and to come home late when she begins her complaints. Their sex life has been reduced to infrequent and unaffectionate contacts.

Just before the husband initiated therapy, the father-in-law offered them a trip to Europe to see if this would help. The wife confesses to have gone on the trip because she wanted a holiday. The husband says that he tried to please her and to pay exclusive attention to her.

The couple has a one-year-old only son. They have a nurse for the child. They waited for some years before having the child because the wife did not want children. Her father persuaded her that because he had no sons he would love a grandson.

The following are excerpts from therapeutic sessions.

Thank you for seeing me. Do you think that she is right, Doctor? She thinks that I don't help her at all and that I

> *don't pay attention to her. She wants me to solve everything. I try, but I can't get my job done and look after the baby. I don't know. I get tired. I guess that I am distant. I try to be affectionate, but I get angry and jealous when she is on the phone all the time to another man. And do you know? I think that he is a homosexual! He is always interested in women's things. He likes to talk about clothes and movie stars and that kind of thing. I don't want to fail in my marriage, but I can't talk like that. It is like my father says. I don't know how to do anything right. She told me to go fix myself up. She won't come because she says you'll make her look like a bitch. I guess it is my fault.*

The manifest melodrama is a sadomasochistic devaluing relationship. John is devalued by his father and his wife. He is accused of being distant and unable to love or satisfy his wife. She threatens him with divorce on the grounds that he leaves her alone and doesn't want to accompany her to parties. He feels inferior to the father-in-law, who provides what he cannot. She places all responsibility for the difficulties in him and refuses to come to consultation.

The patient may compound his position by "fooling" the therapist into believing that the false problem of a sadomasochistic escalation is the cause of his suffering.

John requests therapy basically to be helped to please his wife in her narcissistic demands. He does not talk about his problems of performance at work. He has accepted a dependent relationship with his father. His work record shows his dramatic problems in the sphere of socioeconomic performance. As well, it becomes apparent that his wife went into crisis when she reluctantly confronted her role as mother.

This melodramatic defense requires the complicity of both husband and wife. They must accept the erroneous definition of the problem and play the sadomasochistic game. If he continues to accept that he is a victimizer, he perpetuates the defense and deepens the problem. There are really two failures and two problems: an incompetence in the politico-economic sphere and in the interpersonal sphere. They are incompetent in their personal projects and also in their efforts at togetherness.

If the therapist accepts only the manifest reason for consultation, and does not detect the latent problem, the pathogenic variable is missed. The couple does not look for the problem where it is; they look at what they are able to detect. They both know what to do to play the interpersonal melodrama. Interpersonal mistreatment is what they can see. They can't see what to do about the job situation. Nor can they see the high parental and personal expectations and the comparatively few resources for achieving them to the degree that they are led to expect.

Specific and General Problem Solving

They are incompetent at problem solving in general, not just incapable of resolving specific problems of caring for a child or being an effective executive. The melodramatic definition of the problem impedes its solution.

From the beginning, the therapist attempts to construct a therapeutic antimelodramatic alliance with the patient and to extend this to the environment (Manfredi 1979). He works to avoid or to break the transference-countertransference sadomasochistic acting of the melodramatic defense. The therapist forms alliances and uses other interventions that favor the opening of the frame. The solutions for resolution of the traumatic incompetence is extraframe. He takes "seriously," but not "personally" nor textually, all that the patient and his environment report. He understands that the patient repeats in the therapeutic relationship what he does in his life in general; that is, act his repetition compulsion.

The first task will be to identify and evaluate the patient's dramatic and melodramatic problem and to determine the diagnosis and prognosis. The "official story" is melodramatic. The actual and untold story is the dramatic problem.

In the case of John and his wife, the untold story is of a social incompetence. John is dependent on his father, who controls by not defining roles. He has not analyzed his job. He has submitted to an inadequate plan on the part of his father. As a result of the analysis, he decides to clarify role definitions and responsibilities with both his wife and his father. He does a market study to determine the possibilities of the business. He puts success in a time frame with measurable forms of determining progress toward the goal. He proposes to his father that he be given a salary and a bonus if his area of responsibility meets its objectives.

On later occasions the dialogue begins to demonstrate the latent dramatic problem of socioeconomic incompetence:

> *I don't seem to know how to get what I want. I would like to be a success. I used to collect coins. Do you know what I did? I took some coins from my uncle's collection. That was when I was little. I needed to have a good collection, and I couldn't seem to wait. I'm like that. I get discouraged very easily. My father always said that I would take the easy way. He warned me about alcohol. He says that I could easily become a drunk.*
>
> *You know, I was thinking about what you said about my anxieties. I do have to learn skills. I went over the analysis that we made of my work with my father. I've got those roles pretty well defined—even my wife is getting to know what I define as my responsibility and what I take to be hers. When my father lays a trip on me, I look to see*

> where he is going wrong. I can actually do what you said and not take it personally. That sure helps!

In a later session:

> I never know what is mine. I bought this computer. It was from the money that I get from the trust fund. Then my father told me that I shouldn't have spent the money, so I brought the computer to the office. It is very helpful there. We can keep track of everything on the spread sheets. My father still complains that it cost too much. Now I tell him that what is important is that we are getting our money's worth. He just wants to feel better by making me look like an inept little boy who spends all his money!

Once the underlying problem and the "official" problem are identified, their chance of resolution depends on personal and community resources: the degree of intellectual, emotional, physical, and instrumental competence to resolve the incompetence. The greater the incompetence, the more serious the problem. The patient is more defensively "melodramatic" in his manifestations of his personality. That is, he is more occupied with the irrelevant question of who is bad or inferior than with getting the tasks of survival completed and then pursuing happiness. He is "content" to distribute unhappiness in an illusory, delusional, and often hallucinatory world. He unconsciously "perceives" the dramatic problem as insoluble while consciously not perceiving it as relevant or important. This was the case of John in his work relations and of Mary in her mother's role.

Next, a therapeutic plan is developed for immediate steps toward long-term goals on the strategic and operational levels. The goal is "ambitious" in the sense of seeking the maximum realization and resolution for the patient in accord with the diagnosis and the resources available. The therapeutic "dream" must be viable and meaningful. The project must count on adequate therapeutic techniques as one of the resources. The problem solving by the therapist becomes a model for the patient to develop his own competence to solve a specific problem and also as a general model of "how to solve problems."

This is exemplified in the case of John, when he is helped to have a way of measuring progress and of analyzing the variables to know what to do and in what order. He is encouraged and helped to see the idea of "a free lunch" or an easy victory as part of the "problem."

Containing the Crisis

Once the survival needs of the patient have been assured, the therapist begins to address the problems that must be resolved to find happiness. In the first stage the acute crisis of dramatic incompetence is contained. It affects the patient in a fundamental way and is the problem that has precipitated the melodramatic defense. The crisis is generally contained by "complementing" and "supplementing." The sadomasochistic manifest problem is contained by conscious "complementary" role playing. The therapist in this case is firm and directive with John. He does not expect the leadership to come from John. He is not sadistically devaluing, but he is taking the complementary role of dominating. Gradually he leaves this role and encourages John to take his own stand and to be democratic in his treatment.

Supplementing the failing efforts in solving the latent dramatic problem is also necessary to temporarily rebalance the system. The therapist obviously does not go out and do the job for his patient. He analyzes and organizes the resources and helps to plan and to bring the resources to bear on finding a solution. He brings the breakdown under control. He has supplemented intellectual, emotional, and instrumental deficits until a minimal level of coping can be returned to the patient. This reduces the anxiety from a traumatic level to a signal level and permits the patient to begin to look at what he needs to do. His defense is reduced as his desperation is reduced.

In the case of John, the therapist takes an active role in the analysis of the work situation. He shows John how to do this. He does not supplement to continue the dependency. He supplements and models to alleviate the acute crisis and to give the skills for better general problem solving.

Why do the patient and his environment insist on defining a dramatic problem of failure as if it were a melodramatic problem of interpersonal mistreatment? Why does he not identify and correct his intellectual, emotional, and instrumental incompetence? The crisis that led the person into therapy usually results from an incisive mutation in the environment. The patient feels out of control. Old solutions do not work. He has been put into his narcissistic limbo, which is then maintained by his melodramatic or telemelodramatic defense, or he becomes "melodrugged." To construct an artificial therapeutic "neoghetto," which permits the patient to reconnect with something that he understands and in which he can function with a certain degree of success, is an urgent tactical necessity. The system must be rebalanced and brought under control before it can be changed.

The crisis is not controlled simply by describing its manifest and latent characteristics. Instructions for its resolution and the "complementing" of the patient in his melodrama restore order and a sense of congruence to his world. The therapist takes a complementary role, temporarily and consciously, to balance the system in order to have conditions for change at a later moment. He plays a complementary role for a therapeutic purpose. The therapist complements in the area of interpersonal power, taking the role of authority with John. He also complements in the area of socioeconomic power, allowing an initial dependence. A certain amount of acting of transference is usually necessary. The "countertransference" role becomes a conscious instrument for giving the conditions that will allow later change by temporarily rebalancing the system with the purpose of avoiding a deepening of the crisis of incompetence.

The therapist can turn to environmental "reorganizations" of an emergency sort. He may counsel and give instructions to the relatives and the members of the intimate environment. If the environment cannot complement and supplement the patient to relieve his acute failure, hospitalization may then be necessary. If the major anxiety continues or if the minor anxiety increases in spite of the supporting environmental interventions, then medication may be necessary. The therapist uses the therapeutic "morphines" until the patient reaches an equilibrium. The drugs, like the countertransference, are not used to help him to escape but to rebalance the system that has become dangerously incompetent. The objective is to reduce the anxiety to a signal level so that the underlying problems can be resolved. This is a first step on the road to recovering the lost dream of transcendence in togetherness.

13

Stepping out of Melodrama

ONCE THE CRISIS has been controlled, the therapeutic work now must move the patient from the melodramatic parareality to the dramatic reality. This is done by developing new competence and metacompetence in solving problems. The patient and his environment must face the dramatic problems. These, if unsolved, continue to produce a traumatic anxiety and perpetuate the need for a melodramatic defense. Treatment consists of a stage of "detoxification" and a stage of control of compulsive behavior and leaving the limbo, to enter into the world of pleasure-seeking. The detoxification period requires the use of decreasing doses of the "melodrama" to avoid a complete decompensation. The "melodrug" is given deliberately and under medical prescription, not unconsciously at the instigation of the patient. The therapist also supplements failing social, emotional, and instrumental functions. He may prescribe their supplemental use on the part of the environment.

With John, "relevant dramatic problems" included all of the problems that impeded his becoming economically "independent." The melodrug was the tendency to enter into a relationship of interpersonal "devaluation" while abandoning the struggle for socioeconomic achievement. This "melodrug" of giving interpersonal domination while accepting socioeconomic dependence was administered deliberately "in small doses" in beginning therapy. The interpersonal and social failures were directly dealt with. He was given assistence in how to relate more effectively to his wife and she, although initially refusing to enter treatment for herself, did accept sessions until she could be persuaded that the object of therapy was not to establish who had failed so much as to establish how to avoid failure. John was given specific instrumental assistance when he was given a model for evaluating and solving his work problems. The therapist would be trapped in the countertransference neurosis if he failed to define the therapeutic role and gave solution to the material and work problems without teaching him the skillls, ending up by devaluing him as incompetent. When this happens a new dependency has been developed, the "psychoaddiction" to therapy.

As the system is actively and deliberately compensated by supplementing and complementing therapeutic interventions, the patient and his environment return to a minimal degree of "normal" functioning. This gives the conditions necessary to confront and resolve the counterproductive state created by the compulsive acting of the melodrama Freud (1915a) would describe this as obtaining conditions to understand and resolve the "transference neurosis" as well as the contaminating "countertransference neurosis." The therapist is trapped within the preconscious frame when he fails to resolve this. The patient looks for his help but also, unconsciously, looks to continue to act his defense. Entrapment in the frame, in the best of circumstances, perpetuates a "meloaddiction" and creates a "psychoaddiction." This prolonged or interminable analysis—the psychoaddiction—has been a factor in reducing the prestige of psychoanalysis. The traumatic anxiety persists in the unconscious, and the need to defend is reinforced. The therapist becomes an accomplice to the escape as the neoghetto becomes the same old narcissistic arrangement between sadist and masochist. The therapist is in the uncomfortable role of one who lives off the unresolved anxiety that he himself perpetuates. He restores an unhealthy equilibrium but does not become an instrument to resolve the anxieties that underly the defense.

Working through the Transference

The working through begins by considering the compulsion to the stereotyped melodramatic defense, which is personal in its style and its details, although universal in its form. As the problem of relating competently to the tasks for fulfilling dreams is further reinforced and deepened by the defense, the patient is further trapped. It is to be expected that he return—or, in Freud's terms, "regress"—to his melodramatic defense every time there is an important therapeutic transformation. The therapeutic change produces a crisis of anxiety with a brief return to the melodrama, the telemelodrama, or to drugs, as the patient is confronted by new, frightening demands. This is especially noteworthy at the beginning of treatment. As effective treatment progresses, the defense is less extreme and less frequent.

The working through of the melodrama is based on the analysis and overcoming of the transference and countertransference. The therapist is constantly pressured, manipulated and acted upon, to assume the melodramatic complementary role. Mary acted upon the therapist in an attempt to develop a complicity with him in her devaluation of John. John tried to have the therapist assume an ever more active role in direct solution of the problems that kept him dependent.

In the passage from the stage of control of the crisis to the stage of working through of the melodrama, the therapist deliberately lowers the "dose" of his countertransferential "acting." He moves the patient to a dramatic alliance in which he begins to confront and resolve the crisis of competence. He leaves playing the countertransferential role, to analyze it. If working through is to be accomplished, the therapeutic setting must be "antimelodramatic." The "therapeutic contract" defines and establishes a therapeutic neoenvironment. Mistreatment, disqualification, and exploitation are impeded, as is the deviation from the relevant problem to the "personalization." Both the repressed actual story and the melodramatic story are dealt with so that the problems that they represent may be analyzed and resolved.

Mary offends with her unfounded accusation that the therapist will accuse. This mistrust is not personal but is a part of her multilated and distorting paradigm of understanding, feeling, and action that she applies to all others, with or without justification and while doing what she expects from the other. She accuses and devalues the therapist without even knowing him. She perceives friends as if they were enemies. John will invite devaluation and will deposit responsibility for solution in the therapist.

In other cases, the therapist knows that a "love-intoxicated" hysterical masochistic patient, who idealizes and falls in love readily, will do exactly this with the therapist. It is what the patient does in the transference neurosis. To the degree that the therapist is able to avoid personalizations and countertransference, he is able to better help the patient elaborate his strong addiction to the repetition compulsion and the acting of the melodrama.

When the patient sees no solution to a dramatic problem and enters into a crisis of incompetence, which can be provoked by environmental or personal changes, he resorts to an acting-out of the melodramatic defense. The "out" refers to the fact that the patient is breaking out of the therapeutic frame and returning to the pathogenic frame. As a result, paradoxically, when there is a therapeutic gain there may also be an increase in the major anxiety that the change produces. That is, new competences are required, and new failures must be overcome. The patient will attempt to avoid the increased anxiety by inducing others, including the therapist, to play the melodramatic defensive game. The major anxiety is then converted into the minor anxiety of establishing who is to blame or who is inferior. The defense temporarily escalates and the patient talks of little else in his sessions.

Mary, when confronted with her tendency to seek solace in her father while attacking her husband for incompetence and abandonment, was finally able to see her own excessive expectations for her performance as the superdaughter. She personalized the interpretation as if it were an attack and escalated her devaluing attacks on the therapist before giving this up as a defense. The minor anxiety produced by acting the sadomasochistic relationship had replaced a major anxiety of confronting and successfully executing her social role as a wife and mother. In

Stepping out of Melodrama

the case of John and Mary, Mary's father had tended to perpetuate her behavior by idealizing his daughter. He fulfilled her fantasies while she remained passively demanding. The father helped to confirm that his son-in-law was to "blame" for Mary's frustration. John's father uses John to give himself a feeling of superiority. He does not really attend to the company. He belittles John. His major anxiety of failure in the socioeconomic field is converted into a minor anxiety of having a dependent son.

In working through, the therapist begins by describing how the patient recalcitrantly executes the same type of melodramatic escape. He describes the sequence of actions and the mechanisms of induction and reinforcement that the patient emphasizes. He describes the environmental role in the melodrama, noting its pressures, reinforcements, and its tendency to confirm the patient's distorted perception of the problem and how to solve it. The time, the actors, and the scenario change but the story, like a James Bond film (Eco 1966), manages to repeat an unchanging relationship between the "good guys," who checkmate the "bad guys" in nine brilliant moves. The outcome is always the same, as is the sequence of interactions.

John begins by consciously attempting to achieve a greater degree of social independence. He undertakes a new job. He becomes anxious, because there is no immediate success. As he feels inadequate, he begins to induce others to take over, an easy task to achieve with his father. As another person takes charge, he is devalued and his feeling of incompetence is confirmed. He then flees from the devaluing other and confirms that he is not an effective person.

Establishing "The Facts"

The therapist "denaturalizes" the defense by pointing it out repeatedly. He identifies the plot, the characters, the action, the sequence, and the outcome. The patient begins to see what is happening in a different context. He can take note of his tendency to apply the same paleosolutions to all problems, new and old. This solution is itself simplistic and rigidly applied. The "problem space" (Newell and Simon 1972) is narrow and relatively closed to new information. The patient begins to recognize his metaincompetence and understands that he is seeing the new problems in an obsolete way. He incorrectly defines the problem. Since he cannot alter his old way of understanding, he resorts to understanding the new as if it were the old.

From the lucid metaconscious position, the therapist points out the individual melodramatic compulsion and its relation to the reinforcing ghetto. In this way, the patient grasps the pattern of behavior and develops a metaconsciousness about how he organizes experience and what his assumptions are. The therapist then gives an explanation for what he has helped the patient to see. To begin an "in-depth" interpretation (Freud 1937b), this melodramatic action must be made clear. The patient's awareness of his behavior prepares him to accept the interpretations and predictions that the therapist now proceeds to offer. If latent content is to be determined by analyzing the manifest content, the therapist and the patient must agree as to what the manifest content is. Now, from the metaconscious, the analyst and his analysand perceive the inverted melodramatic intraframe representations, the superficial unconscious direct melodramatic representations, and the repressed pathogenic crisis of incompetence in the deep unconscious.

Having established the sequence of interactions, John, with the help of the therapist, perceives that he is assuming that the dependent state is all that he can achieve. He is unconsciously accepting and assuming the role of "inferior" that he fears to be true. This is the unchallenged intraframe preconscious constriction that makes his feared inferiority and incompetence become a fact. When he undertakes a task, he fails to define his own role and responsibility in realistic terms. He accepts that others (wife or father) whom he perceives as "superior" evacuate their sense of inferiority onto him. He accepts criticism and accepts unrealistic expectations without defining roles and responsibilities. His superficial unconscious contains the direct representation that the other is an "inferior" who deposits his anxieties about inferiority in him. This correct unconscious perception of the other as a depository of inferior feeling does not bring a solution or success. The game of defensive devaluation must be left behind, and solutions must be found for the real problems that stand in the way of personal project achievement.

Only minor resistances are found when the descriptions, predictions, and explanations are maintained within the preconscious frame of who is projecting inferiority feelings. Major anxieties are provoked when the patient tries to leave the melodramatic defense, attempting to recognize and resolve the problem of dramatic performance. Here the patient must recognize significant environmental and personal change and act in accord with the new problems and new potential solutions of a new environment. He must pursue the goal of happiness in the face of a failure that may temporarily threaten survivial. John must do much more than recognize his father-wife's feeling of inferiority, identified projectively in him. He must face his own difficulties in persisting in a task until he is successful. He must develop skills that allow him to be successful. He must confront his father in the business or leave it, since it is doomed to failure if father and son play a game of superior-inferior rather than attending to the real problems in the way of success. John and his father must face the problems of defining his job, doing a market study, standing the anxiety produced by any new business—which will have a normal period of "failure" to produce enough for costs until it becomes established—controlling expenditures, analyzing production and marketing problems, developing sales strategies. If they are to deal with the failure, they must avoid converting the dramatic problem into a defensive problem of the losing game of establishing who is the inept inferior failure.

Reintrojection of the Projected

Profound interpretations—explanatory and predictive—depend on the resolution of the defense mechanisms. They are used to escape into limbo from the intolerable lucidity. The work begins with a de-alienating and repersonalizing maneuver to counteract and resolve the defensive inversion of identities provoked by the projection and introjection of the melodramatic addict.

Now the therapist proceeds to the reintrojection of the projected. For example, Mary, who is the sadist, is shown that she is the "victimizer" in the sadomasochistic defense. Her actions of narcissistic demands for attention while fleeing the mothering role are compared with her words that she is the victim of a husband who does not help her and who will not assume his role. John is made to see that he has projected his victim role onto his "father-wife" while assuming the role of victimizer.

The introjected is reprojected or correctly identified as "outside" and a part of the identity of the other. The sadist sees the masochist as a masochistic recipient of victimizing action. The masochist deidealizes or realistically dequalifies the overqualified and idealized other. John requalifies his wife and his father as insecure people who are not superior to him. The overqualification had led the patient to confuse enemies with friends and to devalue his own contribution. Masochistic John, who was devalued, is revalued by the other and by himself. His contributions are recognized. Parallel procedures are done with the sadist: he must deidealize himself and revalue the other.

Recentering on What is Displaced

With this, the melodramatic splitting between "superior or good victims" and "inferior or bad victimizers" is resolved. The masochist's tendency to polarize positions into a choice between an egoistic superior position or a self-sacrificing inferior behavior are addressed, and the option of a healthy cooperative and mutually respectful behavior is incorporated into the world of possibilities. The displaced is "re-placed" as attention is returned to the problem of a dramatic incompetence. The melodramatic problem is identified as such. Finally, the repression is lifted, and there is a clear analytic metaconsciousness of the intellectual, emotional, instrumental, and physical incompetence that provoked the failure and which had been repressed in the deep unconscious. The lifting of repression is complete when the "naturalized" constricting preconscious frame has been "denaturalized." The frame is opened.

John is able to see that he and his partner must become competent and not simply denounce the failure. The defensive game must stop, and they must seek happiness in the active pursuit of the desired.

In this way, we have traced the therapeutic path from indolent limbo to competent lucidity (see Fig. 13-1).

If in-depth therapy is to be effective, the interpretive work must be realized in an antimelodramatic therapeutic frame. The intraframe, intrapsychic mechanisms of defense can be objectively measured in observable performance.

The therapist is able to use instructions formulated from his predictions of the stereotyped melodramatic defensive sequence. The therapist "proscribes" the melodramatic escapist performance. He "prescribes" the dramatic performance. The patient begins to "unlearn" his melodramatic escape, both within and outside the therapeutic sessions. The therapist may use escalations of the sadomasochistic game to force the patient into the uncomfortable position that he generally leaves to the other. He "outsadists" the sadist in order to make him conscious of the roles in the game. This is a temporary measure, which is not of itself curative. After metaconsciousness is achieved, the paradigm of the game—not just the roles—is what must be changed. These instructions can be reinforced by the therapist's antimelodramatic and prodramatic reactions. The therapist does not limit himself simply to not

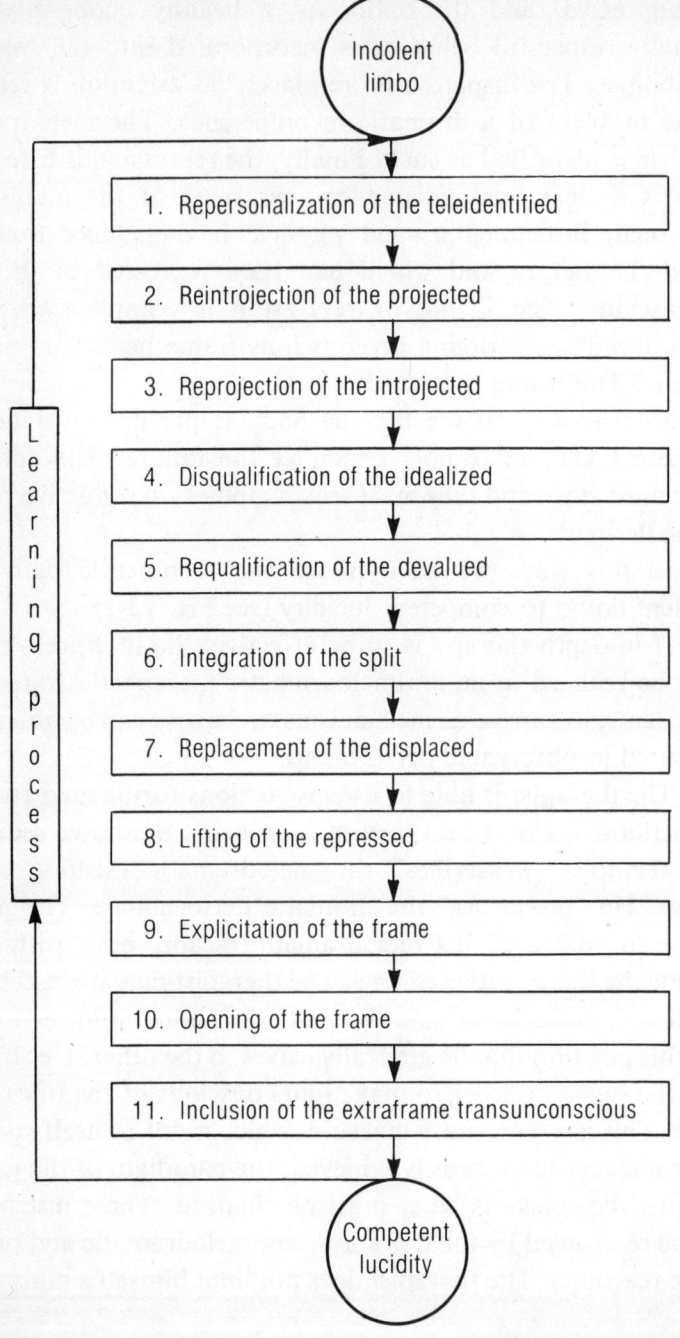

Figure 13-1 From indolent limbo to competent lucidity

react in the melodramatic form; he pro-acts and reacts in a way designed to solve the problem.

In John's case the therapist predicts, interprets, and proscribes John's tendency to "run away from the problem" by changing jobs on the macroscale and by not coming home after work on the family level. He induces his wife's sadistic devaluing and displaces attention with his "diversionary action" from the dramatic failure to a melodrama.

He prescribes that John analyze his work performance to clarify his deficits and to learn new skills. He models problem solving for him and supervises his efforts at problem solution.

He models better ways of handling the wife's sadistic devaluation by not "personalizing" when he is attacked in couple therapy.

This descriptive, interpretative, instructive, and therapeutic stance has a fundamental objective: to help the patient leave the old melodramatic game and enter into the therapeutic game. He stops his escape from unhappiness and begins to produce happiness. This requires the development of new behaviors, both in the individual and in the pathogenic environment. The patient must suffer a revolution, which has emotional and social costs. If he is able to pay the price of the structural change, he becomes able to achieve meaningful transcendence in togetherness. He must exchange his melodramatic escape for a certain inevitable discomfort implicit in the search for happiness. That is, the "illusion of no cost" and the "illusion of impunity" are just that—illusions.

Transforming the Meloenvironment

This elaboration and "unlearning" of the patient's melodramatic individualistic repetition compulsion cannot be maintained if he persists in his unchanged narcissistic environment, his ghetto. The meloenvironment pressures strongly to maintain him in his old behaviors. Although there may be a qualitative changes in the structure and functioning of a system, there is no stability in the new state if the environment does not also change in its structure and functioning. The system regresses to its old meloenvironment.

As a result, working through the individual melodrama must be accompanied by a therapeutic "restructuring" of the environment. Its members must stop functioning as pathogenic melodramatic accomplices and must begin to function as therapeutic allies in problem solving. They are no longer reinforcers of the defense but have become co-therapists, promoters of healthy resolutive behavior.

Since both John and Mary are dependent economically on their parents and both fathers are powerful factors in the environment, it was necessary to include John's father and father-in-law in therapy. The father was given a specific proscription in relation to the use of irony or sarcasm, his two most frequent forms of devaluing. The father-in-law was forbidden to overprotect and indulge his daughter. His competitive behavior with John was pointed out. It was suggested that he give praise only for specific accomplishments. If these environmental changes are not achieved, the couple will be submitted to strong pathogenic pressures. Drug addicts, children, psychotics, and dependent personalities are unable to induce change in the environment, since they are relatively powerless. The environment does not change without presenting major and minor resistances. Just as working through the melodramatic compulsion looked to create new personal choices in the neomind, so the therapeutic restructuring of the ghetto seeks to create new environmental opportunities.

Selecting Resolutive Allies

In this restructuring it is necessary to begin to differentiate which of the melodramatic accomplices are rescuable and which are not. Who are those who will become co-therapists and who will oppose the healthy changes? The environment tends to be recalcitrant. Feuerstein (1980) exemplifies the environmental resistance to intellectual growth in the profoundly retarded in spite of the obvious benefits of change. The selection between the recoverable accomplices and those who will probably not change must be done diplomatically, since most of the members are intimate family and friends. When the patient is required to evaluate and to accept that some of his loved others must be left out of the endeavor, he becomes more realistic. He stops asking of others what they cannot give and does not give to them what they cannot appreciate. He establishes the best relation possible with them; one that, although not productive, will be less "toxic."

Indirect Environmental Interventions

Once the rescuable members of the ghetto are selected, therapeutic rehabilitation begins. This can be done indirectly through the patient, who induces changes in them. If the patient lacks leadership skills or power, this can become the work of the therapist. Here, the individual therapy must be complemented by environmental therapy. Basically the ex-accomplices who are potential allies are given advice in the form of suggestions, prescriptions, and proscriptions to help prevent or reduce the melodramatic acting out and to encourage the specific environmental therapeutic action. Indirect environmental therapy is realized through "supervisions" that the therapist undertakes with the patient. He orients the patient in terms of the best ways to stop inducing his melodrama or accepting the melodrama of others and just what his options are to avoid entrapment in the ghetto. He shows the patient how to behave in a resolutive manner and to induce others to do the same. The "analysand" must become more than an "analyzed"; he must also become an "analyst." He becomes an active agent of mental health (Freud 1937). At the same time, direct environmental intervention transforms significant others in the patient's life into cotherapists in favor of survival and happiness.

Distancing is possibly the most sensitive aspect in this therapeutic restructuring. This is some form of uninvolvement with the nonrescuable members. It may be declared or undeclared, partial or complete, permanent or temporary, physical or psychological. Antimelodramatic "otherectomy" (Gear et al. 1983) has a high personal, emotional, and social cost. The cost factor must be continually evaluated to determine whether the patient and his allies are able to pay the price. If the patient cannot distance himself or reform the ghetto, then therapeutic work is limited to a restitution of equilibrium with slight modifications but without structural change.

Restructuring occurs by combatting the preexistent melodramatic coalitions. New resolutive coalitions are developed with those who are rescuable. A restructuring implies not only a radical modification of the interpersonal microenvironment but also of the politico-economic microenvironment. Some patients need to go through institutional transformations, or leave them, change their work place, community, or even the country of residence.

The Therapeutic Goal:
A Strategic Decision

The therapist should avoid the pathogenic acceptance of an inherently unachievable goal and accept the best possible therapeutic objective. Under the most favorable of circumstances, therapeutic competence will allow for a qualitative transformation of the patient and his environment. The therapist should also realize that at times he will not be able to operationalize his project and will have to settle for a rebalancing or a slight change in the pathogenic and pathological relations between the patient and his environment. The therapist realizes that later relapses are probable. However, circumstances change, and later attempts might allow for a therapeutic transformation from a melodramatic performance within a defensive ghetto into a dramatic performance with a resolutive command group.

Part IV

THE PREFERRED PERSONAL OPTION

14

Implementing a Meaningful Project

WHEN THE CRISIS of incompetence has been controlled, the melodramatic compulsion worked through, and the narcissistic ghetto restructured, the therapeutic work focuses on the breaking through of melodramatic frame constrictions. The therapist points out and interprets the melodramatic defense to bring this to the patient's consciousness. He makes the patient aware that the preconscious melodramatic frame has a pathogenic narrowness, is closed to new information, and is rigidly defended against any questioning. From this frame the patient looks through a "narcissistic window" that provides a narrow view of a limited world. From here he perceives and melodramatically interprets his relation with others and the socioeconomic world. His narrow view does not allow him to see other possibilities to change the individualistic escapist game.

Frame Analysis from "Above"

The patient needs to acquire an explicit critical clarity in relation to this implicit scheme for organizing his thoughts, feelings, and actions. A "denaturalizing" of the "naturalized" paradigm must first take place. The restrictive preconscious frame is examined from "above" (Greimas 1966), as perceived from the metaconscious space. It is a vague set of convictions, distortions, prejudices, myths, and suppositions that he learned and accepted acritically as a child. This melodramatic preconscious "pet theory" is shared by the others in his micro- or macroenvironment. It was transmitted by his family and his society, and it serves to convert information into a socially shared understanding. Without clear realization of what his assumptions are, the patient is forced into a limited choice of options. As he begins to perceive the melodramatic frame and not just the rules of the melodramatic game, he is in a position to question the game itself. In this way, the patient is able to realize that he uses an obsolete counterproductive "theory of relations." This is essential to having the choice of a better game to play and not only to play a bad game better. If there is no metalucidity, the patient, the environment, and the therapist are trapped within the shared melodramatic constrictions.

The first step in opening the intraframe spaces to transunconscious "inclusions" is a "denaturalizing" of the preconscious frame through explanations. Inclusions may then be incorporated, as information is perceived in a more open and flexible way. The neoparadigm is a paradigm better able to solve problems and provide self-awareness and heightened knowledge of the environment. In the now accessible transunconscious space there are various kinds of data that have not been incorporated into the system of understanding. There are neutral data to which the patient has been exposed, although they may be perceived as not relevant and given no affect significance. As the problems of the environment change, they have become important for problem solution in the struggle for survival and happiness. There are other data to which he is exposed and which provoke a value judgment, making their incorporation into action plans impossible. They are perceived as "against" the values held by the system. Potential data not yet experienced but now recognizable will be actively searched for in the transunconscious as his frame changes and he faces new problems.

In-depth interpretations of the working through of the melodramatic frame awaken major resistances. The denaturalizing explanations and the enriching inclusions into the psychic space provoke anxiety and suffering. To go from what the patient thinks, feels, and does to what he does not — or even cannot — think, feel, and do implies a dynamic structural reorganization. Such a change is not a variation of what exists; it is a mutation. Significant others of the personal microenvironment and the shared macroenvironment will aggravate this resistance as their shared understanding is threatened.

The Motivational Switch

During the breaking through, paleodreams are reframed into a transcendent achievable form. This implies a radical motivational switch. The patient must inevitably experience an affect reorganization. Emotions that were attached to the melodrama must be realigned to the productive neodream.

> For example, a talented masochist young musician wants to enjoy and share the fruits of her talent. Her mother has never missed an opportunity to tell her that she is a boastful exhibitionist. Every time she shared her accomplishments, she was labeled as "bad" because of her enthusiasm. The envious mother insists that her sacrifice gave the daughter her chance. The musician does not enjoy success. Her efforts become more directed at assuaging guilt. She is compelled to think about her sacrificing mother and is depressed and ineffective. Her endorphines are diminished. Her transcendent dream of musical achievement has been displaced and replaced by the "melodream" to be a good and humble daughter to her "poor sacrificed victimized" mother. She has become discouraged. Her attention is directed toward avoiding mother's disapproval rather than producing, enjoying, and sharing success. As she is able to denaturalize her shared assumptions and free herself, she will see that a reward is a motive for achievement; that her mother is not a sacrificing victim but a disturbed accuser. The preconscious

frame is broadened and reorganized. The productive personal project is released from a sadomasochistic perception. Affect is realigned. She continues to have the project of becoming excellent in her field. She would also like to please her mother but will not accept a sadomasochistic definition of how to do so. These desires are deeply bonded to affect and to motivation. They have been realigned as a part of her new identity. She has a new frame, a new dream, and a nonmasochistic personal project to be shared.

This crucial emotional therapeutic switch is not produced without psychological suffering. It implies a change in assumptions linked to historic affect. The roots of the patient's identity are here. These are the early fixations described by Freud (1895). In this phase of therapy the therapist either directly or indirectly helps the patient and his environment to bring about the necessary emotional "unbonding" from the sadomasochistic melodream and "rebonding" to the reachable romantic dream.

Socially Shared Pet Theories

The breaking through of the intrapsychic melodramatic frame must be accompanied and reinforced by a breaking through of the melodramatic environmental frame. The musical daughter, if she continues to be exposed to others who confirm that she is an inconsiderate and boastful child, will make an unstable therapeutic transformation. Others punish if the shared paradigm is not accepted. The family myth must be meta-analyzed, as must be that of the larger social order. The patient must either change the environment or find another way to deal with it if therapeutic gains are not to be lost.

Not only must the patient know his personal philosophy of life, he should also acquire a progressive consciousness and metaconsciousness of the environmental philosophy that is imposed on him by his accomplices in the narcissistic game (Glauser 1978). This is a necessary step if the patient and his allies are to generate reachable dreams with viable options for their fulfillment. At this point the narcissistic ghetto is transformed into a constructive neoenvironment from which the patient begins to benefit because of its protherapeutic consensus. This allows the redefinition and metadefinition of the nonmelodramatic paradigm that will more competently resolve problems. The new paradigm needs to be bonded to affect if it is to be motivating. With this, a meaningful dream of transcendence in togetherness replaces the pathogenic unreachable dream that was experienced in a state of shared loneliness.

Challenging the Value Qualifications

Possibly the most difficult moment in therapy, where resistance reaches a maximum, occurs when the therapist questions the patient's dogmatically held value system in what Freud (1923) called the superego, which has governed in an unquestioned way. This implies a metaethical questioning of the sadomasochistic ethic that is implicit in the preconscious melodramatic frame. For example, the rules praise masochists while punishing their actions, and condemn sadists while rewarding their actions. If questioned, the superego punishes even more severely. This system was considered an absolute, not an ethical code among other possible systems of valuing.

Therapy questions the unquestionable. Here the therapist resists strong pressures, since he will be judged "from inside" and will have to handle disqualifications and accusations of a personal and moral sort when he challenges the rules.

In the example of the musician, the mother will become hostile to the therapist and will consider them both "ungrateful"—or any one else who does not see her as the "sacrificed victim." The attack is not personal. Anyone who claims a different view will be disqualified from within the sadomasochistic game as "bad." The therapist must clarify with the daughter that the mother is not a good sacrificed person while the daughter is bad. The mother is frustrated in her own development and envious of her daughter. This clarification is not a moralistic counterattack. It is information that will help the daughter act in a more healthy way with her mother. At this point of challenge to the shared pet theory, the macro- and, most especially, the microenvironment, will likely become hostile toward therapy. A meta-awareness and a position of analytic neutrality will help the therapist. He must avoid becoming trapped in the ideology of the melodramatic simplistic distortion of "good" and "bad," moral and immoral.

Therapeutic Triangularizing

Breaking through implies "opening." It is at this moment that the bipolar dilemmatic scheme is "triangularized" to include a "third" class of possibilities. Hegel (1947) would say that the subject passes from one thought, one sentiment, and one action to a divalent state in which the thesis gives way to the antithesis and, beyond the two, the synthesis that contains both and surpasses each. The two notions, that of "defense" and "deficit," are integrated. Therapeutic "triangularizing" permits solutions to the new and complex problems of the changing reality confronted by the patient and his environment. They can competently cope with those reality shocks that previously would have precipitated a crisis of incompetence.

It is proposed that the classical working through of the desires and the unconscious defenses, characteristic of traditional psychoanalysis, be complemented with the work of "breaking through" the preconscious frame and then with the "working out" of the preconscious deficits in performance (Gear and Liendo

1979) on the conceptual, emotional, instrumental, and even the physical planes. This approach was described by Reuven Feuerstein (1980) in his program to overcome deficits of the mentally retarded.

Traditionally, there have been two types of approaches within psychoanalysis. One was the "psychoanalysis of the unconscious"—developed predominantly by the European disciples of Freud, such as M. Klein, W. Bion, J. Lacan, and so on. Their work centered on the elaboration of the conflicts experienced by the ego as the superego confronted the impulses of the id. The other was the "analysis of the preconscious," eventually called "ego psychology," initiated by Anna Freud and especially developed by her American disciples, such as H. Hartmann, E. Kris, M. Loewenstein, D. Rappaport, and others. Their work focuses on the elaboration of the ego strengths, weaknesses, and mechanisms, and the like. In particular, the conscious, the preconscious, and the ego were analyzed, leaving somewhat to the side the analysis of the unconscious and the conflict between id and superego. The paradigmatic psychoanalysis proposed here integrates the two approaches. We would suggest that a forced choice between the two creates an unnecessary problem. The most effective therapeutic choice would be to include the analysis of the ego, and the conscious, preconscious, and transunconscious, especially in relation to deficits, and the analysis of the superego, the id, and the unconscious, emphasizing defenses.

Dealing with Defenses and Deficits

The concepts of deficit and defense are central. Defenses are unconscious resistances to what one consciously desires. Deficits are incapacities to do what is consciously desired. Defenses are unconscious conflicts between the id and superego. Deficits are conscious and preconscious and have to do with ego. The deficits result from a distorted organization of what is known or what is needed and not yet known. To use an analogy, hysterical blindness is a defense. The patient does not "see" because of an unconscious conflict. Physical blindness is a deficit. The patient cannot see in this case because he has a physical deficit, not a conflict. The lack of a clinical distinction between unconscious defense and preconscious deficit has contributed to serious and frequent therapeutic errors. The therapist may, without being aware, propose unreachable therapeutic dreams. He then might reason that the patient did not reach the goal because of an "unconscious conflict." In fact, the patient may have been deficient in the necessary thinking, feeling, and acting skills.

The nonpsychoanalytic therapist tends to think in exactly the opposite manner. He believes that the patient is not instrumented when the problem is a conflict. He unconsciously does not act, because this would provoke traumatic anxiety and create conflict. These therapists try to teach what the patient and the environment are actively motivated "not to learn." They forget that "There is no deafness greater than that of he who does not want to hear."

Working Out

Upon completing the working through of the unconscious defenses and the breaking through of the preconscious frame, and the working out of the preconscious deficits, both the melodrama and the predisposing dramatic deficits are overcome. It could be said that the working out is etiologic therapeutic work, while the working through was, up to a point, only symptomatic. Paradigmatic psychoanalysis proposes not only to resolve the melodrama; it addresses the incompetence that triggered the defense. A pathogenic environmental situation creates a crisis of incompetence that precipitates an escalation of defensive melodramatic behavior.

The working out focuses on conceptual, emotional, and instrumental deficits that impede resolution of new problems. The patient at this phase of therapy is still unable to do what is now desired: transcend in togetherness. Working out centers on the solution to certain concrete problems that the patient brings to treatment, such as marital difficulties, interpersonal problems, problems at work, and the like. Analyzing how the patient addresses these is part of working out. This phase passes from solving problems to problem solving. The patient examines how he defines problems, generates options, makes choices, and plans. Finally, he studies how he responds to feedback and modifies his plan in accord with the results.

Acquiring problem-solving capacity brings the competence needed to conceive and enhance the process of dream fulfillment in togetherness. Working out the deficits that impede problem resolution prepares the individual to manage a more creative and productive plan.

This broadening and enriching work on the psychic and performance levels needs to be completed and reinforced with a building up of new allies who share healthy desire.

During this phase the patient improves his interpersonal skills to obtain intimacy and togetherness and to stop being mistreated by the melodramatic use of interpersonal authority. There is a reduction of dependency, monopolizing control, or restricting insufficiency in relation to politico-economic control. Deficits are overcome by helping the patient find the manner in which to make an intellectual, emotional, and instrumental enrichment. Of course, a great deal of working out of the problem-solving deficits is realized during the therapeutic process and within the therapeutic setting. Some working out occurs through an extension of the therapeutic process to institutions, such as family and workplace, which may favor his certain specific areas of incompetence.

Through the therapeutic relationship, the patient receives a certain emotional and intellectual support that aids in building up competence. The ability to resolve problems is increased in the therapeutic and extratherapeutic environments.

The following case illustrates this.

Rachel is a high school teacher. She consults because she is depressed and is always fighting. She is married to an alcoholic who is in a crisis as a result of a drinking bout. She is unable to form a consensus with her own family to confront George about his drinking. George drank from adolescence and smoked pot when she knew him as a childhood sweetheart. Her family history includes a father who was an alcoholic and from whom the mother was divorced when Rachel was 8 years old. The mother then married a very severe and controlling man who was abusive to the children. Whenever Rachel denounced the new father for these abuses, she was punished by the mother for causing trouble, while the mother did not react against the father. Rachel would harbor resentment and would again explode when his behavior became intolerable. She would again be called the "cause" of the trouble, would feel guilty, and become depressed. The same pattern is happening with her husband, who gets on very well with her mother. He is quiet and does not fight or denounce. He makes it apparent that he is "suffering" from the abuse of an excessively nervous and exaggerating wife and tends to induce others to criticize the wife while minimizing his problem.

Rachel describes herself as tense and a "fighter." She is extremely responsible and is appreciated at work for her efficient and responsible behavior. She does have problems with resentment. When a friend is hurt by another, she defends the friend, who later pardons the person who misbehaved while she continues to take an unbending and unpardoning attitude. Then she feels left out and betrayed.

She complains that although George is still functioning well at his work as a technician, he does not make any decisions at home in regard to money or children. He comes home, begins to drink, and after a while becomes very aggressive and abusive toward her. He is verbally very depreciating and expresses a great dissatisfaction with her as a woman, as a mother, as a professional, and as a companion. He slams doors, paces, and screams. This offends and frightens her. The next day she is angry and he remembers nothing.

> *My mother says everyone has problems and why do I make such a scandal! She says he is a good provider and I am exaggerating! She tells me, "Be happy. Let him alone. You're looking for perfection. He is so good in other ways. What can you expect? You are such a complainer.*

In this case there is an important interpersonal incompetence on her part at home, in friendships, and at work. It is as if she perceives her instrument of putting a thing right to be "denouncing" the problem to the person or to a higher authority (mother) who is able to do justice. Somehow saying the truth in a loud voice is going to set things right. In fact, she tells people—mother, husband, enemies of her friends—truths that they don't want to hear. The effect is that she is attacked for her interference and offensive clumsiness. The situation becomes worse. Her observations, although true, are moralistic. The other denounces her and is the offended one. She becomes lost in a melodrama of "denouncing the guilty" while she cannot stop the behavior that is causing her real suffering. The historic origins of this losing melodrama are apparent in her family. He who is lucid and denounces the misbehavior is qualified as destructive, whereas he who destroys is tolerated. In the politico-economic sphere, she tends to overassume responsibility. She makes all of the family decisions. She is overloaded as a result of assuming the work of others at school. This again leads to denouncing the irresponsibility of others, while she continues to be resented for her clumsy interpersonal behavior.

The crisis of incompetence (her husband's uncontrolled destructive drinking pattern and her inability to form alliances and to communicate this in a way that favors its solution) is balanced with the intervention of the therapist, who serves as a lucid witness. He confirms that Rachel is correct—that there is a grave drinking problem for which she is not "to blame." He supplements her deficiencies in communication and problem solving. He complements her in the interpersonal in that he accepts her early inability to talk without blaming or feeling blamed. He consciously acts the countertransference in the initial stage, "blaming her for blaming." The melodramatic compulsion is identified in its sequence and worked through.

The restrictions of the frame are pointed out in its pathogenic narrowness of "bad" abusers and "good" abused. The position of not accepting abuse and not clumsily and abusively denouncing it is offered. The behavior of the other is not personalized, nor is it accepted. It is firmly dealt with and limits are placed such as "If you drink, I will not live with you because this causes me pain and is destructive to me. I will not assume the responsibility of stopping your drinking. I will not control you. I will simply take responsibility for my own right to happiness. Neither one of us is to blame. The issue is not who is guilty but what are the conditions needed for my happiness." The ineffective moralistic perception is broadened. There is a breaking through of both the interpersonal paradigm of sadomasochism and the socioeconomic paradigm of control–dependency.

Working out was achieved with the help of rehearsals, and modeling in regard to how to handle communication. Moralistic qualifications and personalization was a clumsy truthfulness. What was to be communicated must be seen to contribute in some way to change the behavior of the other. Truthfulness was not qualified as an absolute virtue.

She develops skills to improve performance. She must improve her intimacy and communication skills. She resolves the sadistic transference with the other, until he develops a relationship of solidarity with her and she with him. This permits them to overcome the hostile shared loneliness. Her emotional capacity for persistence is good, but her husband is lacking in emotional strength. He is actively included in therapy both for her and in his own right. If he is to avoid regression, his wife must also abandon her complementary interpersonal masochism. She must help him talk about the plans to end his drinking and to confront his fear of taking responsibility. She must begin to requalify her own contributions.

Using Strengths

A schematic enunciation of strengths and weaknesses in the four areas of performance does not imply that all patients are a complex of weaknesses nor that treatment transforms patients. Each patient and his intimate others of the microenvironment have a series of specific strengths and weaknesses. The working out of this incompetence concentrates on overcoming these deficits and stimulating and playing into the strengths. Part of Feuerstein's success consists of reinforcing strengths, not just overcoming weaknesses. To use a medical metaphor, treatment of a hemiplegic consists of mobilizing the nonparalyzed side as well as avoiding the harmful contractions in the affected side. The hemiplegic's battles are won on what he has that functions, not just on what is lacking. Developing preexisting strengths helps to compensate weaknesses. This is important if the therapist is to avoid entrapment in another unreachable dream. The "art of the best possible" is what must be learned through the full use of assets.

The Command Group

Generally the nucleus around which the resolutive neoenvironment is constructed is formed by friends and relatives rescued from the "ghetto." In addition, the patient selects new people to create a neoenvironment. He also looks to connect with a macroenvironment that offers new options for transcendence in togetherness. The allies who participate in this "command group" must, above all else, have a disposition to confront relevant problems of survival and happiness. This requires a continuing transformation of the subject in his relations with self and environment.

When Edward Rochester is interviewing Charlotte Bronte's Jane Eyre for the position of governess, he is impressed by her tenacity, essential to success. Talking about her survival in an orphanage for eight years, he says: *"You must be very tenacious to life. I thought half the time in such a place would have done up any constitution!"* The development of these new alliances is not done as if utility were above human worth. Usually the desired moral and personal attributes are themselves reflections of what is basically sought in the alliance: intelligent altruism.

In the next chapter we enumerate some specific conditions that these allies need in order to handle interpersonal authority, their politico-economic control, their analogic or digital coding style, and their level of abstract functioning. The strength of the neoenvironment will depend on relations of complementarity and symmetry between partners. The relations of authority, politico-economic control, and level of abstraction should be symmetrical. The digital and analogical style should be complementary. Strengths and weaknesses complement one another so that deficits that cannot be personally overcome can be compensated by the strengths of others who, in turn, have weaknesses that are supplemented by other group members. A certain access to politico-economic power makes transcendence possible, as does the adequate handling of interpersonal power. It is this which makes togetherness possible.

These resolutive alliances of the "command force" in the neoenvironment must be capable of mutual help. When one falls into the temptation to play the melodrama, others function as co-therapists who intervene in the face of the temporary regression.

They put the group back on task. The patient and his group help one another as they all become agents for health.

To build up the micro- and macroresolutive neoenvironment, alliances must be formed and the patient repositioned in the existing politico-economic environment. If this is impossible, then a new politico-economic structure is sought that offers more effective options for transcendence. The patient ought to be in a position to relocate himself in the power structure of his work, community, country, and so on.

Next, it is necessary for the patient to develop his capacity for alliances based on intelligent altruism. He must no longer confuse enemies and friends and must leave the melodramatic enemies of mental health to form dramatic productive friendships that favor health. The patient puts distance between himself and his potential melodramatic accomplices, whether these be sadists or masochists. He needs allies who favor his competence for facing incompetence and who do not enter into a defensive alliance at the first sign of failure. He will develop stable and firm coalitions for mutual help, sharing this on the level of intimate power.

The therapist will not only function as a key transitional figure and in the structuring of the redimensioned neomind with which the patient plans his neoperformance. He will also be important in the structuring of the corresponding neoenvironment. The environment has been transformed from an accomplice in defense to an ally in dramatic endeavors. It helps to resolve the problems creatively and constructively instead of perpetuating escape.

From Indolent Limbo to Mastered Reality

The steps of the therapeutic work begin by a diagnosis of the patient's dramatic problem in his environment. A strategic and operational plan for treatment is drawn up. Therapy continues

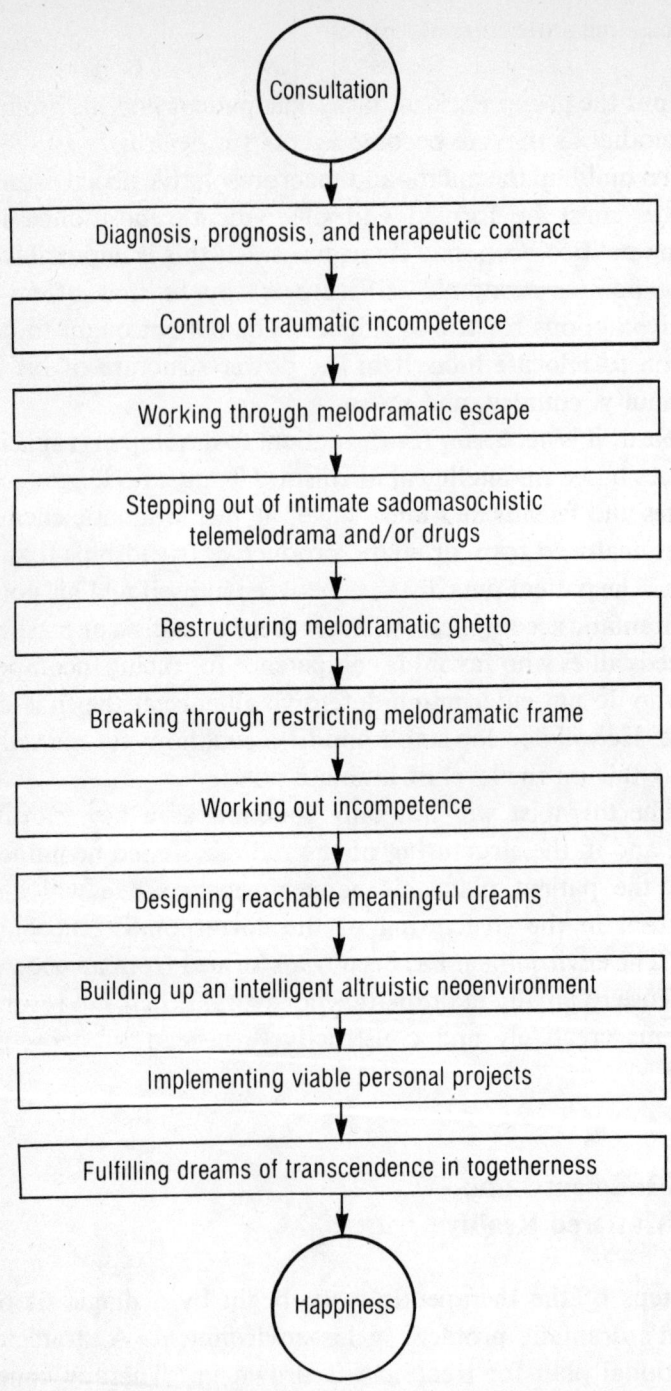

Figure 14-1 The therapeutic option

Implementing a Meaningful Project

with the control of the crisis of incompetence which is the "untold repressed story" of the first consultation. Once the system has been rebalanced and the daymare is over, working through begins on the individual melodramatic compulsion. At the same time, the narcissistic ghetto is restructured in the interpersonal and politico-economic dimensions. Then the breaking through of the restricting intrapsychic and environmental frame is undertaken.

Once the patient has broken through, he enters into the working out until he overcomes or compensates the deficits that produce his incompetent performance. Once this therapeutic operative is reached, conditions must be developed for its maintenance. That is, a command force of intelligent, efficient, and committed allies is developed to help achieve the personal project. Optimal conditions have been carefully structured for producing happiness for self and others (see Fig. 14-1).

15

Strengths, Deficits, and Project Realization

15

Strengths, Deficits, and Project Realization

WE NOW STUDY four psychosocial parameters especially relevant in a therapeutic restructuring of the ghetto. They are observable in the discourse and actions of the therapist, patient, and members of his environment and are useful in establishing guidelines in the selection of a creative and productive "command group" of committed allies and in selecting a couple relationship. The parameters are: the cognitive "style," the "level" of symbolic abstraction, politico-economic "control"—the handling of institutional power, and interpersonal "authority"—the handling of intimate power. Their systematic application allowed the creation of four clinical typologies.

The typologies have been found useful in determining the strengths and deficits of a given patient. They are a factor in his capacity to negotiate desire fulfillment within the limitations of his environment. Two of these parameters with their typology are described for the first time in this book. These are cognitive style and level of abstraction. The other two, interpersonal domination and politico-financial control, are the subject of a previous book; the reader is referred for detail to *Patients and Agents* (Gear et al. 1983).

Cognitive Style and Personality

Sperry (1973) put forth evidence for two forms of cerebral functioning, distinct but complementary. They seemed to reside in the two distinct cerebral hemispheres. The "silent" right hemisphere had tasks different from those of the "talking" left hemisphere. Although both functions are present in all people, many do have a marked predominance of one hemisphere. Its imbalanced use seems to result in a particular cognitive style. As well as affecting how they symbolize, it affects how they learn, feel, think, and act (McCarthy 1980).

This typologic classification between analogic right and digital left personalities has its roots in ancient philosophy. The Greeks made a great distinction between the "Dionysians"—synthetic analogic thinking right dreamers—who differed markedly from the "Apollonians"—analytic digital thinking left dreamers.

Durant (1976) writes:

> In effect, they spoke of two gods. At first there was Dionysus (Bacchus) the god of wine and revelry, of ascending life, of joy in action, of ecstatic emotion and inspiration, of instinct and adventure and dauntless suffering, the god of song and music and dance and drama. Then later there was Apollo, the god of peace, leisure and repose, of esthetic emotion and intellectual contemplation, of logical order and philosophic calm, the god of painting, sculpture and, epic poetry. The noblest Greek art was a union of the two ideals. The restless power of Dionysus inspired the chorus; and Apollo the dialogue; the chorus grew directly out of the procession of the satyr-dressed devotees of Dionysus; the dialogue was an afterthought, a reflective appendage to an emotional experience.

This dichotomy in styles led to the postulate that there are two general complementary types of personality, the "right brain" or "analogic" and the "left brain" or "digital." To have a predominantly right brain analogic style implies looking for a complementary left brain digital partner. He will have strengths where his partner has defects.

Strengths, Deficits, and Project Realization 179

The right dreamer uses images and analogies. His thinking tends to be associative, inductive, and generalizing. He is emotional, creative, and interested in possibilities but is disorganized on the level of operations. He learns by experience. The left dreamer is factual and verbal. His thinking is logicodeductive and tends to precision and detail. He is interested in getting the job done but is not interested in creating new possibilities. He is operationally oriented and disciplined. He learns by instruction.

The following description is of a typical "analogic" style:

Ed is an architect. Design is his specialty. He works with another architect, who likes to do the calculations. He is very creative and always open to new experience. His problem is that at times he is too open and changes his ideas drastically. His curiosity is insatiable. He has explored eastern religions and dislikes dogmatic positions. He is very sensitive to others' feelings. Such topics as the meaning of life are brought to the consultation and discussed with passion. His hobby is painting, and he is particularly good with color. He is affectionate but he considers himself unlucky in love, since he has had three unhappy marriages. He tends to initially idealize his partner and to become rapidly and deeply involved. He discovers that his love is not as he thought and he has to abandon the relationship.

The following is a part of a session:

Ed: *I felt the music in her voice. It was warm and sensuous. I knew at once that she was a woman of deep emotions. I have been inspired since I met her. I have painted nothing but blues and reds since we started going out together. What do you think? I'm scared. Is this the right one or another mistake?*

In response to this analogic, imprecise, intuitive evaluation, the therapist focuses on the deficit, supplementing the digital capacity of his patient.

Analyst: *You ask me to decide because you are unable to be sure on such vague information. Until the data are more precise, the uncertainly continues and you either make an unfortunate decision or you impulsively act and again repent at leisure. You need to analyze the situation, asking yourself what is the information that would be pertinent. Do you remember what we talked about when we identified your deficits? What I suggest is that you establish the facts. You needn't stay with your intuitions and feelings.*

An example of a digital personality follows:

Ruth is the wife of an alcoholic. She is very concrete and explicit. She requests exact instructions from the therapist.

Ruth: *I want to know exactly what to do. I don't want any vague statements. I want to know whether I should leave him. He's drinking again. Next it will be cocaine. I'm not putting up with it. He is irresponsible and he fools himself, but he isn't fooling me any more.*

As well as being digital she functions on a low level of elaboration. The therapist replies, trying to help her to grasp the context and to understand that there are situations that require time to define themselves. The establishment of limits and a time frame for results allows a more effective definition than simply threatening to leave. With this intervention, she is taken to a higher level of digital thinking.

Analyst: *Ruth, it would be valuable if you could put this problem into context. You tend to threaten and not to carry through. I can understand your anxiety that things are creeping back to where they were. Possibly, if you can clarify for yourself the minimal conditions necessary for you to stay with him, and the time that it will take to develop the optimal conditions that you desire, you will both have a clear idea of what is a good action plan and a way to measure progress.*

Coding Level

It is important to relate and combine the typology based on cognitive style with another that is derived from three coding levels or "degrees of symbolic elaboration" conventionally used by the individual, although not the only level on which he can operate. Understanding of reality is organized in a process that passes from the more concrete experiential levels to the more abstract levels of the principles involved. When we refer to "level of abstraction," we are not simply describing intelligence. University graduates may become accustomed to limiting the elaboration that they give to their experience. It is as if the person is somehow limited to use a certain level, even in the cases where he has a greater symbolic potential.

During the process of developing a system of organized "understanding," there is both an analogic and a digital representation possible in a progression from the concrete to the abstract (Prieto 1966). The process of symbolization is related to the capacity to perceive and unite through the detection of similarities and to perceive significant differences. This is the child's base for establishing categories and then patterns. He also organizes by opposites, contrasting high with low, large with small, and so forth. Affectively, he divides the world into that which favors and that which threatens survival, and then he links it to the pleasurable and the agreeable. That which threatens survival is extremely anxiety-producing. Beyond this, that which fulfills desire is pleasurable and that which frustrates desire is unpleasurable. The motor for action becomes the seeking or avoiding of a certain emotion in accordance with the affect organization of the symbolic system.

The elaboration may be done in a principally right-brain analogic style, relying heavily on examples and images and emphasizing similarities; or it may be done in a principally left-brain digital style, relying heavily on logical processes and emphasizing more precise distinctions (Bruner 1964). The person begins his organization of experience and its affect significance by establishing an analogic representation, a diffuse "prototype." This vague and general prototype is then explicitly digitalized into a more precisely detailed formal category. On all levels, the "analogic" form of representation is more open-ended, vague, like a "fuzzy set" or an intuition, being implicit rather than explicit. On the middle level of elaboration and unification, experience is integrated across time. Repetitions are detected analogically as "patterns." These are then represented digitally in "laws" which take a more explicit and precise form. On a still higher level, the patterns and laws are integrated into a broader frame. More complex relationships are established between different patterns and laws to include an organized "meaning" and certain predictable correlations. These are the "paradigms" or the "informal" explanatory examples. The paradigms are formalized and expressed in words as "complex systematized theories." On a still higher level of integration, an even broader understanding is formed. This allows the person to capture the "gestalt" on the plane of the principles that organize his thinking and to metathink about his thinking. On this level the person develops an understanding of himself as the experiencer in a specific context of culture and personal circumstances. This full elaboration and integration allow a maximum usefulness to be derived from raw experience. In effect, to the degree that the subject reaches more abstract levels of refinement in understanding the world, the more likely he is to be successful. One of the objectives of psychoanalysis is to develop the metacapacity to perceive oneself and analyze one's perceptions; that is, to metathink about thinking.

The elaboration of symbols passes through all these steps when the symbolic world is well developed. In an arbitrary division of this process, there are those who make a predominant use of one of three levels: the high, middle, and low. From this may be derived three types of personalities: the high, or "highlanders"; the middle, or "flatlanders"; and the low, or "lowlanders."

A high-level personality, or "highlander," is characterized by a strong interest in the establishment of gestalts and general theories and looks for contexts and principles on a metatheoretical level. Understanding is broad. Concern is for the long term. The "highlander" is strategic, quick to understanding, and able to retain detail and complexity, highly integrating his ideas and including a consideration of the context. He usually enjoys and understands a good sense of humor (see Fig. 15-1).

A medium-level personality, or "flatlander," centers his interest on the establishment of patterns, laws, paradigms, and simple theories. Concerned with the middle term, he is a tactician, slower in understanding. He simplifies by not taking complex interrelations into account, more than by searching for uniting principles. Thinking is undervalued.

A low-level personality, or "lowlander," has an interest in the individual case. He is circumstantial and concerned with the immediate. He is simplistic in his understanding, losing a grasp of essential interrelations and relevant detail. Strangely, at the same time, he may be trapped in an excess of irrelevant detail. He usually does not consider the context before giving meaning to his experience. He has no sense of humor, and he doesn't understand subtle jokes. The example of Ruth on p. 180 is typical of a low-level coder.

Six Types of Dreamers

The typology based on analogic and digital style acquires greater applicability when combined with levels of abstraction — high, medium, and low. From this combination results a typology of six clinical categories or six types of dreamers. These are the digital high, the analogic high, the digital medium, the analogic medium, the digital low, and the analogic low. Each one has a particular mode in which he conceives, perceives, and acts in his search for happiness and in the meeting of his survival needs. Having defined the characteristics of the six types, we will demonstrate how their strengths and foibles work in their alliance or complicities.

The Analogic Highlander

The analogical abstract coder shows openness, creativity, and capacity to synthesize in a rapid and pertinent form as his most relevant virtues. He is very comfortable with and competent at the combination of new theoretical modalities and in the generation of new explicative paradigms. He is more interested in the consistency of his models than in the disciplined application of the rules

RIGHT ANALOGIC	LEFT DIGITAL
Synthetic	Analytic
Tendency to omnipotence	Realistic
Self- or other-devaluing	Evaluates nonjudgmentally
Emotional	Deliberate, unemotional
Uses metaphor and analogy	Speech precise and factual
Intuitive	Logical
Theoretician	Relation of theory to action
Fascinated by possibilities	Values achievement
Charismatic leader	Democratic leader
Strategist, operationally weak	Strategist, operationally strong
Playful	Very adult
Rebels at routine	Accepts routine
Idea person	Doer
Unconcerned about appearance	Attentive to appearance
Enthusiastic but inconsistent	Consistent and persistent
Rich inner life	Rich, productive life
Undisciplined in health habits	Disciplined in health habits
Heart disease	Dyspeptic

Figure 15-1 The highlanders or analogic and digital abstracts

of correspondence or the pragmatic implications of his model. He tends to be a lucid strategist but a relatively inefficient tactician. His lack of consistent discipline and his fascination with new ideas tend to make him prematurely abandon his own action plans. When a hypothesis cannot be rapidly implemented or does not produce immediate results, he does not look to review tactics and persist in actions. He simply develops a new theory. He tends to be a charismatic but inconsistent and inconstant leader. He is not good at giving detailed explanations to others, which would allow a greater understanding of his position. He tends to see the other, who is slower to grasp things, as a more "stupid" and inferior being. He tends to have misunderstandings with his significant others as a result of this. He tends to be a brilliant investigator and theoretician but a poor teacher. He has more time for ideas than for people. Paradoxically, he is a solitary individual who does not like to be alone. He is a manic-depressive personality.

The following is a history of a high analogic personality.

James is the principal shareholder in a consulting company established by him four years previously. He is enthusiastic and is very quick to define and understand the complex problems of others' companies. He is, however, uninterested in routine or in the control of details. His partner is also a creative, imaginative, but undisciplined person. They have managed to have excellent ideas and quickly see the potential in the innovative. As a result, they have moved quickly to become the representatives of foreign products and programs that have proven to be very popular with their clients. In spite of their great talent, the company is unable to solve its own routine problems of billing, personnel development, and the like. The partners do not take an interest in these areas and are bored by the discipline necessary to manage their own company. In their consulting work it is enough to offer a brilliant solution. The company organizes the application of the solution. They go on to another problem. Not only do they not have skills or motivation in the area of operational routine, they actively devalue these skills.

The analogic abstract tends to complement himself with a digital abstract or a middle-level digital partner. These personalities help him to organize himself, improve the clarity of his communication with others, and deal with the pragmatic need to achieve socioeconomic goals.

In this case leadership and power were very strongly in the hands of the analogic highlanders. Although this worked well on the level of the actual consultations with other companies, it was not adequate for the smooth functioning of their own company. Analogic highlanders are not good leaders in the routine area. Their strength is creativity and openness to the new. They have deficits in the area of logical sequential ordering and in staying sufficiently closed to stay on track. The digital highlander is more deficient in the creative area.

The Digital Highlander

The digital abstract personality has the capacity to formalize, synthesize, and reformalize theories. He is interested in meta-theory and in logical congruence. He tends to behave as a democratic but somewhat rigid leader who is able to understand and to operate on the principle of reciprocal altruism. He is slower to capture ideas than is his complement but is more consistent, organized, and persistent in the application of these ideas. He compares the desired results with the actual outcome and reviews the problem on a tactical and technical level, rather than discarding the theory. From the point of view of human relations he tends to give an image of an objective, rather cold, and distant leader. He tends to be somewhat schizoid in his personality. (See Fig. 15-1.)

James and his partner hired a very competent digital highlander, Jean, who is good at organizing and able to provide a consistent democratic leadership. She is persistent and consistent in her efforts. She sought psychotherapy because she was unhappy and contemplating a change in employment. Her reasons were that when she tried to become precise and arrive at an agreement with her employers, they became evasive and jumped on to other topics, never really deciding anything. They did not value or give priority to such things as her billing plan. She felt that her talent was underutilized and undervalued. She could not stand their inefficiency. She was increasingly frustrated in her plans and derived no pleasure from her work. She did not have the power to make the decisions necessary to save her projects. She wanted to be sure that her proposed change of jobs was necessary. There was very little melodrama. She did not blame her bosses. She simply found the situation nonfunctional. She had identified her dramatic problem and wished to analyze her alternatives and to see what in her had made her have this same type of difficulty before in the last consulting firm, which she had left for similar reasons. Her excellent coding capacity and her tendency to control her emotions had kept her relatively on task.

The Analogic Flatlander

The middle analogic tends to be dramatic and emotional in his communication. He gives more importance to emotions than to events. He performs satisfactorily in relation to his interpersonal relations. However, in spite of being agile in this area, he tends to be less effective in the achievement of his politico-financial objectives. He is a seductive and demagogic leader. He tends to experience a sense of claustrophobia when he has to persist in the pursuit of these politico-financial goals. This tends to make him an activist who is not always productive. Although he is very much in touch with himself and others on an emotional level, he tends to generate a great deal of anxiety in others because of his tendency to change his plans and to flee. He is a hypomanic personality who is less effective than his hyperactivity would seem to imply. He often has a very good degree of enthusiasm and is energetic. He has a tendency to promiscuity. (See Fig. 15-2.)

RIGHT ANALOGIC	LEFT DIGITAL
Dramatic	Moralistic
Emotional, empathetic	Cold, aloof
Dramatic, nonverbal	Matter-of-fact, verbal
Sweeping overgeneralizations	Precise, narrow-minded
Great precision creates anxiety	Lack of precision creates anxiety
Claustrophobic	Agorophobic
Ignores significant, relevant detail	Too much irrelevant detail
Intuitive	Legalistically logical
A people person	A task person
Feelings, not facts	Facts, not feeling
Seductive but frigid	Potent but nonseductive
Unfaithful	Faithful
Overweight	Underweight
Human relations	Productivity

Figure 15-2 The flatlanders or analogic and digital mediums

The following patient is an analogic flatlander:

Peter is a very charming young man who is in public relations in a large company. He has very good interpersonal relations and is sensitive to the feelings of others. He has such jobs as taking out the visiting dignitaries. He tends to drink to excess and has been involved with various young women.

His reason for consultation is that his wife has found a lover, and this has made him desperate since he now realizes that he is in love with her and does not want to lose the children. He confesses to have spent a great deal of time out at night. He now laments this with a great emotional show. He recognizes that his wife cannot count on him. His company does not pay well, but it has put him in touch with many opportunities with clients. He has ideas but has never acted on these and has remained in his old position. His work performance exploits his strengths as a "people person," but his lack of persistence and his tendency to move away from serious involvement and to expect instant emotional gratification has made intimacy difficult to achieve.

The Digital Flatlander

The digital of middle level has narrow criteria and tends to behave rigidly in accordance with the law. He tends to be morally judgmental. That is, he is a predominantly paranoid personality. He likes to give and receive absolute instructions that are invariant in their application in spite of differing circumstances. He is persistent but is productive in the politicoeconomic sphere as a result of his strong bureaucratic inclination. He tends to be dominating in the interpersonal but has little dexterity in producing an environment of intimacy, since he is rather clumsy and aggressively sincere. At times he is called a "porcupine" because he is clumsily direct.

Just as the analogic of middle level tends to be dominated irrationally by his emotions, the middle digital tends to be dominated by his rigid rules and compulsions that transform him into someone so serious that he does not enjoy a sense of humor. (See Fig. 15-2.)

Geraldine is an executive and a divorcee. She has carried forward many large projects and has been recognized for her efficiency. She is, however, a very unhappy young lady. She feels like a failure in the interpersonal field. She has not found a good couple-relationship and has been hypercritical of those with whom she could have considered a relationship. She is direct and disagreeable but feels she is being frank and sincere. An older man, a widower, approached her with romantic interests. He was a respected professional consultant to her company. She told him that he was too old and not really very interesting as a person. When invited by him to visit his house, she told him that his taste was very middle class. In his presence at a cocktail party she told the president of a rival company that his product was inferior and should be taken off the market. It is not surprising that she had difficulty in couple-formation. She is excessively outspoken and at the same time is very sensitive to slights.

The Analogic Lowlander

The concrete analogic is someone who is impulsive and whose actions are dominated by a lack of tolerance to frustration. He acts and reacts without much reflection instead of observing a strategic plan. He is particularly incapable of anticipating even the immediate consequences of his acts. He does not assume responsibility for consequences of his acts. He is short term in his plans and irresponsible in his behavior. He depends on others to neutralize his failures. That is, he uses the other in an insensitive and manipulative fashion with a curious capacity to seduce him and make him excessively responsible. His personality is psychopathic with a marked tendency to escape frustration by using such things as drugs.

The Digital Lowlander

The sixth type of dreamer, the concrete digital, tends to be literal and to be very dominated by irrelevant detail. He is rigidly attached to simple routines that require an inflexible totalitarian organization imposed by others. He tends to be of an obsessive compulsive personality type. He looks to others to develop strategies that he can execute in a rigid way. Since he does not really understand or take into account the context, it is impossible for him to be creative and imaginative. He can, however, execute stereotyped routines developed by others.

Just as impulsivity and irresponsibility were characteristics of the low analogic, the literality, rigidity, slowness, and excessive irrelevant detail are the characteristics of this group.

> Betty is a very careful person who likes to have everything quite clear. She thinks in "black and white terms." When faced with a problem, she goes over the same information an infinite number of times. She takes things quite literally and doesn't change her decision when the context changes. She has extreme difficulty in synthesizing and in grasping the whole picture. Her husband is a very absolute and dictatorial man. She is very submissive to him and does not question his orders. She comes to consultation because she is having difficulties with her work. She has a new boss, and he expects more initiative from her than she is accustomed to. This has made her anxious, and she is sure that the boss will find her work unsatisfactory. She is falling behind in her schedule because the more anxious she becomes, the more she gets lost in irrelevant detail.

The union between a concrete digital and a middle digital tends to achieve a certain degree of symmetry in that the middle digital gives explicit and detailed orders, which the low digital requires. They function in the world of projects to be achieved, but they do not achieve a satisfactory degree of intimacy.

Politico-Economic Power

The third parameter for establishing a healthy productive relationship with the environment is the handling of politico-economic power, or "control," extremely important to dream fulfillment in the area of "transcendence." Politico-economic incompetence is usually accompanied by a secondary interpersonal problem with intimacy. Togetherness cannot be developed, because the patient "defends" from the anxiety of politico-economic failure, using an interpersonal melodrama. Helplessness produces a nightmare or daymare. This is the topic of a previous book by the authors. Statistically, it has been shown that level of income is one of the factors that most influence the type of dream that a person can conceive and aspire to fulfill. Relief from economic worry increases the quality of sex and opportunities for intimacy.

In terms of politico-economic control and productivity, personalities could be classified as "solvent" and "insolvent." Those who are solvent are not judged so simply because of economic resources but on the ability to identify, confront, and resolve politico-economic problems cooperatively. This usually increases resources. The solvent personality would be a "solvent solver" in an interdependent pattern of relationships with another. When there is a need, one of the partners can assume responsibility for the other. Circumstances determine the temporary loss of symmetry. The relationship tends to be democratic and flexible.

The pathological group—the insolvent personalities—can be subdivided on the basis of excessive monopolies or restrictions regarding confrontations in the politico-economic arena. A monopolistic asymmetrical distribution of control yields two subtypes of insolvents. The monopolizing "agent" controls and manipulates, making others dependent. The complement of the controller is the dependent "patient," who induces the other to take politico-economic responsibility for him. When the strategic solution to insolvency is restrictive in the handling of the limited politico-economic resources, there is restricted insufficiency. Christopher Lasch (1978) in the *Culture of Narcissism* describes our times as the age of diminishing expectations. People are barely self-sufficient and reject the idea of looking after others. Those who are insufficient represent a variation of the "individualist."

They cannot construct great projects, and they lack a solid sense of togetherness. Scarcity-conscious insufficients are restrictive in the distribution of the politico-economic control.

This typology is the topic of *Patients and Agents,* and the reader is referred to this for a more detailed treatment. This parameter is illustrated with two cases in the next chapter, which are analyzed in terms of the four parameters for classification that have been represented here.

Interpersonal Authority

The fourth significant parameter is the handling of interpersonal authority. The positions are egalitarian, dominating, or dominated. Personalities can be classified into two types: the democratic and the totalitarian. In an intelligent democratic relationship, both positions are of mutual respect, help, and stimulation. The relations thus established with others tend to be symmetrical. The totalitarian personalities that tend to show a marked asymmetry in the management of authority can be predominantly dominant and sadistic or submissive and masochistic. The sadistic totalitarian personality mistreats, disqualifies, and exploits others within certain limits. The masochistic totalitarian personality, complementarily, is mistreated, disqualified, and exploited. When the sadist and masochist are talking about themselves, they perceive and talk "in reverse" to how they act. The totalitarian sadist perceives himself as mistreated while he mistreats the other. The totalitarian masochist does the opposite.

From the perspective of handling authority as well as control, symmetrical alliances seem to give the better prognosis in performance and intimacy. The democratic nonabusive personalities dedicate themselves more to the task, are supporting, qualifying, and constructively critical. The totalitarian personalities tend to defend melodramatically. The symmetrically totalitarian sadist with a masochist tends to be stable but not intimate. The most unstable and counterproductive couple would be two totalitarian sadists or two totalitarian masochists.

The Power Typology

Combining the pathological types derived from the management of politico-economic control and interpersonal authority, we would have six basic types of personalities (Gear and Liendo 1980). There are "sadistic agents," who control and dominate; "masochistic agents," who are controlling but are dominated; sadistic patients, who dominate but are controlled; sadistic insufficients, who are restricting and dominating; masochistic insufficients, who are restricted and dominated, and masochistic patients. Examples of this pathological distribution of power lie in the couples formed by them. It is possible to establish some relations of correspondence between the diverse clinical types of personality derived from combining style, level, control, and authority. For example, the sadistic agent tends to be a high digital; the masochistic agent, a high analogic; the sadistic insufficient, a middle digital; the masochist insufficient, a middle analogic; the sadistic patient, a low analogic; and the masochistic patient, a low digital. This is an approximation, not an absolute. Solvents tend to be high democratic. The masochistic agents tend to be demagogues or charismatic leaders of medium to high. The insufficients tend to be authoritarian lows and medium. The low masochistic patients are authoritarian. These correspondences are really schematic, and other combinations are frequent.

16

Treatment Strategy Based on Strengths and Deficits

COMBINED WITH OTHER clinical data, the typologies described in Chapter 15 permit a more specific prediction of the outcome of personal projects and of the quality of the patient's interpersonal relationships. They are factors to be supplemented or corrected if they represent deficits and to build upon if they represent strengths. They are considered in the selection of couples and allies and in structuring the therapeutic environment. If it is possible to predict which alliances will be successful, the patient and therapist are able to establish or select the micro- and macroenvironmental relations that have the greatest promise of happiness.

These four parameters have influence on the success or failure to establish an intimate interpersonal relationship.

Style Complementarity and the Couple

The left brain personality tends to form an alliance with the right that gives them more possibility of success. Although the analogic and digital personalities perceive and interact with the world in two distinct styles, they need and fascinate one another (Bogen 1969). "Opposites do attract," but to get along implies that there be basic similarities that make for compatibility and understanding. The complementarity of styles must occur within a shared social paradigm and a similar context. The lack of cultural similarity usually overrides the importance of a complementarity in style. Togetherness is difficult to achieve if the pairs are not complementary parts of an integrated whole symbolic social code. This is seen in transcultural marriages, where thinking styles are often complementary but the preconscious suppositions are distinct. They do not operate on the same assumptions or place the same value on certain behaviors.

A case history illustrates therapeutic implications of the typologies.

> Tommy is a mathematician. The theoretical aspects of his work are fascinating to him. He is a renowned professor, bold in his contributions and in the public positions that he takes. His outstanding theoretical contributions brought him to the attention of people in government, and he was offered a position which required that he apply his theory and that he organize and direct a large number of subordinates. His tendency to become bored and to abandon routine, to be more fascinated by a new idea than by its disciplined application, to be impatient with those who do not grasp at once, all contributed to a crisis of competence in his new job. Socioeconomically he had been successful in other jobs more suited to his strengths and less demanding in the area of his deficits. He tended to be indifferent to socioeconomic power and to overvalue "intellectual" power.
>
> His handling of the interpersonal tended to be absolutely demagogic. He expected admiration from others and tended to make promises that he was not disciplined enough to fulfill. He could be clumsily disparaging toward the powerful if he considered them to be slow. He considered himself superior and them inferior.
>
> In the personal area, his marriage had been in difficulties because of his impatience and his tendency to devalue his wife, whom he had threatened to leave.
>
> The wife, Susan, is medium-level digital personality. Even if she does not enjoy routine, she has unassumingly

undertaken all routine tasks, protecting him from the demands of children and household. She does not attempt to comment on his ideas or to develop ideas of her own. She likes exact answers given to her by another. Rules and order give her a sense of security. She is slow to grasp things, but persistent. Her reasoning is logical, and her speech tends to be about "facts," not feelings. She has a much greater capacity on the operational level, but this is not given the importance that it deserves, either by her or by Tommy. Her level of functioning has deteriorated during her marriage as she has become accustomed to simply carrying out his desires.

Tommy is an analogic highlander. His strengths are his creativity and his rapid grasp of complex problems, which he is able to model analogically. His interest in theory is accompanied by deficits in the digital area. He does not put into effect his operational plans. He deviates from his objective. As is typical of his typology, he confuses the slowness of the other in reaching his conclusions to the other's supidity. Tommy's creativity is an asset that requires that the other be effective on the operational level if they are to get the job done. His complement, Susan, has a discipline that is helpful in running the household and helps her to follow through.

Tommy's high level allows the therapy to use interpretations and complex explanations. His tendency to devalue requires that the therapist assume the role of expert. His deficits are identified, and he is offered two possible strategies: that of complementing himself or that of assuming a greater responsibility for his self-organization. He was shown that his tendency to disparage and his interest in new projects without finishing the old made him unable to progress on the book he wished to write. Two factors were identified. His expectations were those of a "golden boy." He must write a brilliant and original book to exceed all others. His expectations were idealized. His problems of leadership were analyzed to see how they were affecting his threatened failure at work, which was the "untold story."

The melodramatic story of marital difficulties was also a serious problem. They had lost intimacy. She had been converted into his "mirror," reflecting his desire. She was not a companion; she was a depository for his inferior feelings.

In relation to the power typology, he is a sadistic agent. He controls the family resources, makes the decisions, does the strategic goal setting, and so on. Interpersonally he is classified as sadistic because of his devaluing remarks to his wife and to others with whom he works. His need to control and devalue was a factor in his wife's deterioration. He often did not spend time with her but would go to visit others to debate theory and for intellectual stimulation that she could not provide.

He needed what he had at home on the job and for the personal project: someone to take over, organize, and routinely apply his theories to leave him free to create models of the economic crises. He has fallen into the "Peter Principle." A move to greater power represents one which requires administrative skills, exactly where he is deficient. He is a theoretician, uninterested in administrative routine. He begins to fail. He was encouraged to find an executive assistant to operationalize the models. If Susan or the "executive assistant" does not take charge of getting things done, the plans stay on the drawing board.

Susan needs him to put zest in life. She is a rather timid person, inhibited about expressing emotions related to joy and happiness, and she is attracted by his uninhibited emotionality. She has no academic pretensions and accepts her role of "stupid." Until it was demonstrated to her that she was capable, she was content to admire him and to remain without a personal project for transcendence. He fulfilled his prophecy that he was accompanied by an untalented "mother-caretaker."

Tommy entered into crisis when he started his new job. He

perceived his wife as not good enough for him and had an affair with another digital partner who complemented him at work. The new partner was not as masochistically submissive as Susan. He needed her to assure his success on the job, doing at work what Susan did for him at home. The relationship was not democratic. He was demanding and devaluing. She was functioning at a higher level of abstraction than Susan, being a digital highlander. She became depressed. She was a masochist but could defend herself. Socioeconomically she was dependent, but valued her independence as a lover. She kept control over her own resources and would not let him make decisions for her.

Therapeutic tasks were defined as identifying, analyzing, and resolving the defensive melodrama of interpersonal mistreatment which defeated attempts at togetherness. The failure at a new task is related to the deficits. These must be corrected or complemented. Tommy's personal project, the writing of his book, must be examined to determine what factors impeded its achievement. Susan must be helped to recover from her devalued diminished state to return to the development of a personal project. She returned to study and emancipated herself from her dependent relationship with Tommy. Interpersonal power, the domination of Susan by Tommy, could be dealt with as her enclosure was broken and as she began to resume a relationship with the politico-financial world, and to demand a share in the decision-making process. The therapist served as the "superego of the superego," requalifying her in the face of the devaluing attacks by the other until she was able to change her perception of herself. In the transference she idealized the therapist. A strong intelligentizing action was undertaken.

In therapy Tommy's transference was manifested by devaluing the therapist and proving his own superiority. The therapist pointed out that Tommy did not know who his friends were and that he did not enter into relations of intelligent altruism. His unresolved competition with his sadistic father was analyzed.

Couples with Symmetrical Styles

The dyads that are both left or both right tend to have the same strengths, but they also share the same weaknesses. They do not compensate one another effectively. Work groups may be all digital and effective at getting things done, but not creative when a new problem arises. A company such as James's, with the power and leadership totally in the hands of an analogic group that reinforces itself in its desire to explore possibilities, tends to fail because of the lack of balance between "imagining" and doing.

Coding Levels and Couple Formation

Unlike the coding styles that are complementary and of equal worth, higher levels of abstraction are more complete, not complementary, to lower levels. The high-level coder uses a more elaborated and integrated symbolic representation of his experience. He is more flexible and maintains complexity. Each type of coding level has different ways of dealing with reality. In the formation of couples, a certain similarity is recommended in the level of abstraction. When there is no similarity, and a high-level coder must live intimately with a low-level coder, the more intelligent is often bothered by the slowness or lack of understanding of his partner. The less intelligent is bothered because the other is "very complicated." Frustration results. This in part was what happend to Susan and Tommy. One of the important therapeutic tasks was to "re-intelligentize" Susan. Possibly, among the most difficult of tasks is living with someone unable or uninterested in the same level of elaboration of experience. It is recommended that highlanders form couples with highlanders or with a partner from a middle level. The middle level "flatlanders" usually function with other middles, although they can function with a high or a low. Unfortunately, the lowlanders often have more chance of being "intelligentized" if they form couples with flatlanders. Unions between high and low tend to be based on pathological needs. Analogic and digital personalities live in different or complementary worlds but use different levels of abstraction.

With couples on different levels, the one with more contact with the world, economic resources, interpersonal authority, and the like influences the less powerful one. In *Smart Hubbies Mean Brighter Future for Wives,* Gayle Young (1987) reports on a thirty-year follow-up study undertaken by Warren S. Chaie of the University of Washington. He reports that when there is a difference in levels there is a tendency to "relevel" to the politico-economically more powerful. The wife of a laborer is less capable, whereas the wife of an executive tends to be sophisticated. The longer that the couples stay together, the more similar they become. This we have found in the democratic couple relations where there is a sharing egalitarian attitude.

The therapist encourages coupling of individuals who are already intelligent or can be "intelligentized." Complementarity in the style and symmetry in the level—or with a maximum difference of only one level—is the most effective combination.

In the case of Tommy and Susan, Tommy had a "deintelligentizing" effect on his partner. Susan had become accustomed to accept his thinking. He did not explain himself in detail, becoming inpatient with her slower and more logical thought processes. She felt unable to understand and accepted his evaluation of her as "an interesting body carrying around an empty head." His nickname for her was "my brainless rib." As a result of therapy she was induced to take up her studies again and to graduate with a degree in administration. She began to enjoy discussions and to show her capacity to think problems through. She became more interesting to him and was able to face her dilemma and look for a "triangularizing" solution which allows an option productive of happiness.

> *If I study, I will be ridiculed as inferior for being so slow. If I don't study, I will be ridiculed as inferior and discarded as uninteresting. Better that I prepare myself and have a potential for achieving my own goals. My object is not to compete senselessly with my husband. It is to prepare myself for greater happiness, preferably with him whom I love, but not at the expense of my own development.*

The therapist was under the constant challenge of "outdoing Tommy." It was necessary to show Tommy that there are two ways of thinking and that although brilliant in one, he tended to depreciate the characteristics of the other. He loved to speculate and to try to understand the problems, but he was not at all enthusiastic about the efforts of the therapist to digitalize him. He was bored by the detailed precision in reasoning and by the routines that must be established to achieve things in the workaday world. His aversion to routine and lack of motivation to explore detail or to put models to the test made him look for his complement rather than developing these skills. He accepted the deficits as the price of specialization. He did, however, learn to follow a strategic plan and to set himself personal goals from which he did not allow himself to constantly deviate. He worked on his tendency to devalue the digital thinker for his slowness and lack of creativity.

The Coding Typology and the Couple

The combination of style with level leads to the six coding types previously described. A complementarity in style seems to be the most effective combination on all levels. A high level in both partners is most effective, since it implies a more complete symbolic elaboration. The couple who are symmetrical at a high level of abstraction and complementary in style, for example the highlanders, have the most opportunity for success in their personal projects and in their togetherness. Right highlander and left highlander complement. The right is creative and is complemented and potentiated by the superior organizational skills of the left highlander. Balance is achieved between dreaming and doing (Torrance 1984).

An alliance between two digital abstract subjects would run the risk of losing creativity and imposing excessive discipline with a lack of playfulness and a loss of the joy and human aspects. They can maintain goal-directed behavior, but often the objective itself is not sufficiently elaborated. They are tenacious, but not flexible or creative. They are efficient, but they tend to concentrate on the material and to lose the flavor of life. They reinforce one another in their compulsivity.

The complementarity between analogic and digital abstracts on the middle level is frequent and fosters a stable relationship. Analogic highlanders often compete with their digital counterparts. When there is a difference in levels, the digital middle level does not compete, but accepts the leadership of the analogic member. This produces less friction but often results in a lower level of intelligent functioning by the middle level digital. In the case of Tommy and Susan this is what occurred.

The alliance between the analogic and the middle digital lacks creativity. In a rather rigid middle class, they are vulnerable to radical environmental changes. However, the analogical helps the digital to escape from routine and imparts to him a feeling of self-worth. The digital provides consistency and control.

An example is found in the case of Dianne.

Peter's wife, Dianne, is a digital flatlander. Peter called her the "iceberg," because she was emotionally very controlled and cold. She did not seem to enjoy things very much and was more of a quiet spectator at the parties that he so often held. He had once become involved with cocaine, and she had struggled to remove him from the company of users into which he had fallen. He gave her life a bit of spice. She managed to keep him from losing all perspective.

Either of these types of middle-level personalities can establish alliances with personalities that are complementary on higher levels. A digital abstract who can perform competently but lacks affect may be complemented by the emotionality and spontaneity of the middle-level analogic. This middle-level personality would not be as creative as his partner, but would be less impatient and demanding of the other, and might accept more readily the control and discipline of the high-level digital.

The analogic abstract may form a couple with the digital middle level, as is the case with Tommy and Susan. Here there is not a threat to the high level analogic's productive capacity. The middle digital would be more disposed to admire and to follow the analogic abstract member. He would obey the orders and leave the higher-level thinker to his abstract ideas. In this way the analogic high level could remain in his ivory tower of imagination while his partner deals with the tasks of the everyday world. The complementarity is an operational alliance where the analogic abstract is the leader, and the middle digital his right-hand man.

On the middle level, the right flatlanders are "people persons," tending to be disorganized but highly developed in interpersonal skills. They are complemented by the left flatlanders, who are rigid and task-oriented. Between them they have the skills to model for and complement one another in the deficient areas.

On a low level, both the analogic and digital coders are easy victims of the overwhelming anxiety of failure. They are more likely to revert to melodramatic or telemelodramatic defense, being at a disadvantage both in the politico-economic and interpersonal aspects of dream fulfillment. They are more concerned with survival than happiness. They are concrete in their thinking. The right lowlander is characterized by his impulsivity, whereas the left lowlander is characterized by his attention to irrelevant detail and lack of a strategic conceptualization of problems. Surprisingly, the right flatlander may be an effective partner for both the right and left lowlander. He tends to be authoritarian and rigid, which contains the impulsiveness of the right lowlander. He also tells others what to do, which makes him complementary to the left lowlander, who wants to be told. These unions function but do not lead to the development of intimacy. A highlander with a lowlander would be bored and boring; the relationship would tend to be unstable. Therapists, employers, and others who form relationships with lowlanders must be more active and must have the resources available to supplement their deficient functioning.

The preferred couple alliance would be that of two symmetrical and resolutive people capable of intelligent interdependence. The least effective combination for projects of transcendence would be two dependent individuals. The most troublesome combination would be two restricted insufficients. The union between dependent patients and monopolizing agents would be negative in terms of transcendence, especially for the dependent patient, but it would favor the stability and tranquility necessary for togetherness. In the unions that are established between patients and agents, the levels of abstraction will be determined by the agent. However, a union between a middle-level agent and a patient of a high level would probably lower the level of functioning of the patient. In this parameter symmetrical relations appear to give the best prognosis with the already mentioned exceptions. Optimal unions require style complementarity, high levels of abstraction, and symmetry in control.

The Power Typology and Couple Formation

The six subtypes of the power typology which results from a combination of interpersonal power (domination) with socioeconomic power (control) tend to form four basic dyadic or polyadic unions: the democratic, the demagogic, the undercommitted, and the authoritarian. The democratic union is between a person who is "solvent," able to cooperate with others without controlling them or being controlled by them, and able to relate without resorting to domination or submission. The case of Jean, who was the digital business consultant, is illustrative. She wanted a consistent democratic leadership, based on egalitarian principle. She found herself with James in a demagogic type of relationship with many promises that were not fulfilled.

A democratic relationship between two solvents permits romantic relations that are stable and satisfactory. The second option would be a demagogic union between a masochistic agent, controlling but dominated, and a sadistic patient, controlled but dominating. This type of union permits intimate stable melodramatic relations. Unsatisfactory options seem to be the most frequent, although not the most convenient. There is an undercommitted union between the restricting and dominating "sadistic insufficient" and a restricted and dominated "masochistic insufficient." Here the difficulty is specifically that it is not possible to depend or be depended upon. It favors unstable melodramatic relations and finally the telemelodrama of being abandoned in solitude. This was the relationship of Edward to his erratic and abusive lady friend. There is a terror that the other will overstep the bounds of one's private life. These people are "alone together" (Weber 1987).

The fourth option, and possibly the most pathogenic, is the authoritarian union between a controlling and dominating "sadistic agent" and a controlled and dominated "masochistic patient." This is the most primitive and obsolete totalitarianism and, as a result, produces the greatest maladjustments, such as psychosis, drug addiction, and the like. In the case of Tommy and Susan, Tommy is a sadistic agent. Although he does not participate in the family work, he controls the resources of the family and considers himself to have the power of decision in regard to economics and the family. He is dominating and devaluing to Susan. She is considered unintelligent and is devalued by him. Susan has developed an increasingly depressed and dependent attitude. The productivity of Tommy is not what it promises because of his operational deficits. As he fails at work, he escalates the sadomasochistic melodrama and spends a great deal of time proving that she is the inferior one.

Possibly the most powerful combination to achieve a meaningful transcendence in togetherness with a resolutive command group in the environment would be complementary in style, high in level, and symmetrical in control and in authority. Within this general panorama, the major option for success seems to be the union formed by a high solvent democratic analogic and a high solvent democratic digital.

The most difficult combination is the symmetry of style and lowness of levels, with extreme complementarity of pathological control and authority. Within this group, the most troublesome would be two low analogic totalitarian sadistic patients or two low digital totalitarian masochistic patients. These seems to be predestined to reach "loneliness in lowland." They do not have intimacy and cannot handle tasks.

Therapeutic Implications of the Typologies

The therapist is not limited with these significant parameters. The therapeutic plan compensates or modifies them.

A therapist helps the patient toward "whole brain" rather than a right or left domination. An analogic or a digital personality is moved toward an integrated one or is compensated in the couple selection. Deficits in levels of abstraction are modified by helping the patient to go from a low or medium level of abstraction into a higher one, from being a lowlander to being a highlander. "Intelligentizing" action requires requalifications, a reassessment of self-worth, a freeing from a hypercritical devaluing other, and so on. The "intelligentizing" action was discussed in detail in the case of Susan.

Politico-economic control is modified by helping the patient go from an excessively monopolizing, dependent, or restrictive relationship to a solvent one. Susan made contacts outside the home and developed greater control over her own life.

An interpersonal democratizing action helps the patient to go from being a sadist or masochist to being egalitarian. The lowest quality of transcendence is found in those who are low-level insolvent and totalitarian. They can only reach a "limbo" or a "loneliness in lowland." The highest quality of transcendence is found in those who are high-level solvent and democratic. They are likely to reach the "paradise" of togetherness in highland.

A case history examines all aspects of the model.

Roland and Aurora are a young couple who have come to consultation for "marriage problems," for which Roland perceives Aurora to be responsible. He finds her cold and unenthusiastic. They had been childhood sweethearts. They were helped economically by his father, who literally supplemented Roland's income, giving them a limitless sum on which to live. Neither one was very effective in the politico-financial world. Roland was an expert in interior design. Aurora had worked as a volunteer. She was an avid reader and enjoyed intellectual pursuits. She had been taken care of first by her own father and then by her father-in-law through her dependent husband.

The couple went into crisis after the death of Roland's father, when the position of the "agent" who looked after problems and gave leadership and direction was suddenly vacant.

Roland was pushed into assuming family leadership, but he was totally unsuccessful since he had been spoiled and protected during his life. His mother had submitted to him and he had fallen into the habit of violent outbursts, threats of suicide, blaming tirades, and the like, when he had to face up to something. He hid his misdemeanors and would blame another when caught. It was difficult to reason with him, since he used words as instruments for getting the result that he wanted. He was totally lacking in consideration, was irresponsible, and used his charm to seduce the other into believing his convenient lies. He seemed to not understand "acting on principle." That things were "correct" or "incorrect" was not a part of his "paradigm." If they led him to avoid personal frustration, the wishes of the other were unimportant. He was "premoral" in his thinking.

Upon the death of his father he attempted to take the family leadership. His mother was ambivalent. With reason, she did not trust his judgment. At the same time she did not want to lose her power. If he had control of the family fortune, she was without power.

Aurora was under attack by him and the mother, qualified in her "ghetto" as the silly little girl who was not able to be an adequate wife. She had a difficult time in establishing consensus because, although very intelligent, she had no leadership skills, and she did not know how to handle his defaming attacks. She would withdraw to the world of philosophy and intellectual studies.

Aurora is a digital thinker of a high level. She is logical, unemotional, and interested in philosophical discussions. She is a masochistic patient who is accused by her husband of affect detachments, of "being the cause" of his nervousness. He "suffers" in her hands. Politico-economically, she is a "patient," being dependent on her husband's family. She works as a volunteer in a kindergarten because she is interested in child development.

Roland is an emotional, erratic, impulsive, imaginative young man who does not learn from experience and does not think about his own thinking nor about the consequences of his actions. His decision are based on avoiding immediate frustration. He operates on the pleasure principle. He is an analogic low-level thinker. He is maintained economically, and is also protected from frustration. He is the "sadist."

The "paleoenvironment" of both was overprotecting and castrating. Socioeconomic problems were solved by the father. The mother encouraged sadism by submitting to abuse and by accepting sadistic behavior to get what one wants. He threatens suicide if he is not gratified immediately. Aurora was taught to accept abuse in order to have security. It was assumed that she did not have to become a family leader. She did not even have interpersonal power, being masochistic.

The crisis of incompetence was precipitated by the death of the father. This represented a "mutation" in the environment. There was no leader and no protector. The "dramatic problem" had to do with what course the family was to follow. Who was to lead? Who had the capacity to confront the world?

The major anxiety provoked by this crisis of competence was converted into a minor anxiety in a "sadomasochistic melodrama." Roland deviated attention from the drama and melodramatically complained about his wife's affect detachment. He converted himself into a poor frustrated victim of his incompetent wife, who was not much of a woman. He repressed and projected his own lack of capacity to feel "manly" and introjected the role of victim. The melodrama, however, guaranteed a return of the repressed. The unresolved problem of social potency continued to threaten the survival of the family. There is a "complicity" on the part of the couple who reinforce this erroneous perception—the wife accepts that she is withdrawn and to blame for her husband's bad feelings. If she were more of a woman, there would be no problem. The mother continues the overprotection, afraid to confront a suicide or other impulsive behavior if she frustrates her son. She also blames the wife and flees from her own responsibility. The "ghetto" consisting of the mother, sister, and brother-in-law operates on a consensus that the wife is a silly little girl to blame for the troubles. Treatment requires that the consensus be changed to favor the wife, who is able to form healthy alliances.

In the transference he blames the therapist for his troubles, saying that he has not changed because the therapist is incompetent. He comes to agreements and then breaks them. The therapist must form a consensus to control his promiscuity and drug abuse. Use of words is beyond the patient's capacity. It is necessary to use the action mode. The "neoenvironment" must have a leader with control and authority. His wife must be helped to assume this role. She must have the support of the mother, who must alter her view of the situation. Socioeconomic control over his part of the family fortune must be transferred to the wife if the fortune is to be saved. She must learn to apply her abstraction abilities to solve the everyday problems of her life.

The therapeutic approach to the wife is more classical. She responds to interpretations and is capable of insight. She is encouraged to give up her habitual way of solving problems, that of being a little girl who must be mollycoddled and protected. She becomes a mature woman and beings to impose limits. He, finding her no longer a depository for his melodramatic accusations and presently a source of frustration, leaves the relationship. Rather than accepting a change in the therapeutic neoenvironment, he constructs a ghetto with another socioeconomically dependent woman who is willing to accept a role of complementing masochist in exchange for economic security.

Aurora successfully negotiated the change, constructed a therapeutic neoenvironment, seeking the counsel of experts in relation to how to manage her situation. She returned to her studies and began to pursue her personal dream of self-realization as a professor of philosophy. Her children became more secure as they were protected from the impulsive outbursts of their father. She had made the motivational switch from accepting blame in order to receive economic protection in a state without closeness or a personal project.

The therapeutic goals in Roland's case had to be limited to a rebalance of the system. There was a real threat of suicide. The therapist must complement him temporarily, accepting the role of the one to blame. When his crisis was contained, his problem of impotence was addressed. He was helped to accept a strong but benevolent and digitalizing father figure who would counsel him and gradually impose greater degrees of frustration, taking him from use of the pleasure principle to the reality principle. Demands had to be gradually increased.

An example of how to reach an integrated, high-level, solvent, and democratic relationship of romantic transcendence is found in the dialogue in which Charlotte Bronte's Jane Eyre redefines her relationship with Edward Rochester:

"Reply clearly," he commands.
"I don't think sir, you have a right to command me, merely because you are older than I, or because you have seen more of the world than I have; your claim to superiority depends on the use you have made of your time and experience."

Jane's reply leaves no doubt as to her firm belief in a democratic egalitarian relationship. She refuses to accept a dictatorial or abusive attitude, or an arbitrary assumption of authority. She simply is not to be dominated. Her answer also reflects her capacity to reason and act on principle.

"You are my paid subordinate, are you? Oh yes, I had forgotten the salary! Well then, on that mercenary ground, will you agree to let me hector a little?"
"No, sir, not on that ground: but, on the ground that you did forget it, and that you care whether or not a dependent is comfortable in his dependency, I agree heartily."

Again Jane accepts her economic "dependency" on Edward as his employee. She does not accept that he abuse this power. What makes her respect him is not the power, but his use of it. He has consideration for an economically "dependent" person. She distinguishes between being affluent — which she is not — and being "personally solvent," which she is. She cooperates in a free relationship. She accepts his proposal specifically because he was

Treatment Strategy Based on Strengths and Deficits 215

not abusive or monopolistic. He did not exploit her "dependent" state.

> "And will you consent to dispense with a great many conventional forms and phrases, without thinking that the omission arises from insolence?"
>
> "I am sure, sir, I should never mistake informality for insolence: one I rather like, the other nothing free-born would submit to, even for a salary."

Jane shows a keen intelligence that clearly and logically analyzes what he is saying. Her command of language, her clear definitions and deductions from facts would tend to indicate that she is a left highlander. She consistently decides on principle and does not simply accept the norms or customs. She puts things in context and is flexible and self-reflexive.

> "You are afraid of me, because I talk like a Sphinx."
>
> "Your language is enigmatical, sir, but though I am bewildered, I am certainly not afraid."
>
> "You are afraid—your self-love dreads a blunder."
>
> "In that sense I do feel apprehensive—I have no wish to talk nonsense."

Edward tends to make intuitive and insightful statements. He uses metaphor. He is enigmatic and often misunderstood. He focuses on feeling. He is a right highlander who complements Jane in her matter-of-fact clear style. As a result of this dramatic redefinition of the relationship, they reach a prototype of a sublime moment of togetherness in highland:

> "I tell you I must go!" Jane retorted, roused to something like passion. "Do you think I can stay to become nothing to you? I am not talking to you through the medium of custom, conventionalities, or even of mortal flesh: it is my spirit that

addresses your spirit; just as if both had passed through the grave, and we stood at God's feet, equal—as we are!"

"As we are" repeated Mr. Rochester, "So," he added, enclosing me in his arms, gathering me to his breast, pressing his lips on my lips; "So, Jane."

The deep bond that Jane is capable of feeling makes this a romantic moment. Togetherness has been experienced. If we refer to the economic analogy from *A Hard Look at Modern Bonding,* (Reinemer 1987) we would consider this a "high-yield bond," where Jane has risked her assets, her principal—but has not lost her principles. She remained true to herself and did not simply look for security. She has sought and given commitment in a fair and intelligent relationship of caring.

It is a few years later that Jane Eyre tells us about the returns on her "investment." It would seem that she committed her assets and took her risks in a "bull market":

"I have now been married for ten years. I know what it is to live entirely for and with what I love best on earth. I hold myself supremely blest—blest beyond what language can express because I am my husband's life as fully as he is mine. To be together for us is to be at once as free as in solitude, as gay as in company. My Edward and I, then, are happy: and the more so because those we most love are happy likewise."

The sharing of happiness has come to Jane. Freud would have said that Eros prevails over Thanatos.

REFERENCES

Allen, W. (1985). *The Purple Rose of Cairo*. Orion Pictures.

Asch, S. E. (1956). Studies of independence and conformity: I. A minority of one against a unanimous majority. *Psychologist Monographs* 10(9).

Aulagnier, P. (1966). *Le Désir et la Perversion*. Paris: P.U.F.

Bayles, M. (1987a). Crass Krantz recrudesces. *The Wall Street Journal*. February.

——— (1987b). TV: big bad businessmen. *The Wall Street Journal*. April.

Bion, W. R. (1962). *Learning From Experience*. New York: Basic Books.

——— (1965). *Transformations*. New York: Basic Books.

Bogen, J. E. (1969). The other side of the brain: an oppositional mind. *Bulletin of the Los Angeles Neurological Societies*. July.

Bory, J. L. (1960). Le roman populaire aime les mythes. *Les Lettres Nouvelles*. 9:135-142.

Bronte, Charlotte. *Jane Eyre*.

Brunner, J. S. (1964). The course of cognitive growth. *American Psychologist*. 19:1-15.

——— (1973). *Beyond the Information Given*. New York: W. W. Norton.

Correale, A., Fadda, P., and Neri, C. (1987). *Letture Bioniane*. Rome: Borla.

Durant, W. (1976). *The Story of Philosophy*. New York: Pocket Books.

Durkheim, E. (1951). *Suicide*. Glencoe, Ill: Free Press.

Eco, U. (1966). James Bond: une combinatoire narrative. *Communications* 8(4).

Feuerstein, R. (1980). *Instrumental Enrichment*. Baltimore: University Park Press.

Fiumara, R., Caporali, M., and Zanazi, M. (1983). Il se e l'identitá. *Il Narcisismo*. Rome: Borla.

Franzt, P. (1976). L'espace dramatique. *Revue des Sciences Humaines*. 41:162.

Freud, A. (1936). *The Ego and the Mechanisms of Defense*. New York: International Universities Press.

Freud, S. (1985). Project for a scientific psychology. *Standard Edition of the Complete Psychological Works of Sigmund Freud*. Vol. 1. London: Hogarth Press.

───── (1900). The interpretation of dreams. *Standard Edition* 45.

───── (1905). Fragments of an analysis of a case of hysteria. *Standard Edition* 7.

───── (1909a). Analysis of a phobia in a five-year-old boy. *Standard Edition* 10.

───── (1909b). Notes upon a case of obsessional neurosis. *Standard Edition* 10.

───── (1910). The future prospects of psychoanalytic therapy. *Standard Edition* 11.

───── (1911). Formulations on the two principles of mental functioning. *Standard Edition* 12.

───── (1912a). The dynamics of transference. *Standard Edition* 12.

───── (1912b). On beginning the treatment. *Standard Edition* 12.

───── (1914a). On narcissism: an introduction. *Standard Edition* 12.

───── (1914b). Remembering, repeating and working through. *Standard Edition* 12.

───── (1915a). Observations on transference love. *Standard Edition* 12.

───── (1915b). Repression. *Standard Edition* 14.

───── (1915c). Instincts and their vicissitudes. *Standard Edition* 14.

───── (1915d). The Unconscious. *Standard Edition* 14.

───── (1916). Some character types met within psychoanalytic work. *Standard Edition* 14.

───── (1918). From the history of an infantile neurosis. *Standard Edition* 17.

───── (1920). Beyond the pleasure principle. *Standard Edition* 18.

_____ (1921). Group psychology and the analysis of the ego. *Standard Edition* 18.

_____ (1922). Some neurotic mechanisms in jealousy, paranoia and homosexuality. *Standard Edition* 18.

_____ (1923). The id and the ego. *Standard Edition* 19.

_____ (1924a). The loss of reality in neurosis and psychosis. *Standard Edition* 19.

_____ (1924b). The economic problem of masochism. *Standard Edition* 19.

_____ (1926). Inhibition, symptoms and anxiety. *Standard Edition* 20.

_____ (1927). Fetishism. *Standard Edition* 21.

_____ (1937a). Analysis terminable and interminable. *Standard Edition* 23.

_____ (1937b). Constructions in analysis. *Standard Edition* 23.

_____ (1938). An outline in psychoanalysis. *Standard Edition* 23.

Ganne, G. (1966). *Messieurs les Bestsellers*. Paris: Perrin.

Gear, M. C., Hill, M. A., and Liendo, E. C. (1981). *Working through Narcissism*. New York: Jason Aronson.

Gear, M. C. and Liendo, E. C. (1975). *Action Psychanalitique*. Paris: Minuit.

_____ (1979). *Sémiologie Psychanalitique*. Paris: Minuit.

_____ (1980). *Psicoterapia della Coppia e del Gruppo Familiare*. Florence: Del Riccio.

_____ (1981). Metapsychology of sadism and masochism. A bipolar semiotic model. *Psychoanalysis and Contemporary Thought* 4:207–250.

Gear, M. C., Liendo, E. C., and Scott, L. L. (1983). *Patients and Agents*. New York: Jason Aronson.

Geluser, D. (1978). *La Naturalization Simbolique*. Doctoral dissertation. University of Geneva.

Goodman, E. (1978). Never enough in money games. *The Daily Journal*, Caracas. March.

Greimas, A. J. (1966). *Semantique Structurale*. Paris: Larousse.

Hegel, F. (1947). *Phénomenologie de L'Esprit*. Paris: Aubier.

Klein, M. (1955). *Envy and Gratitude*. London: Tavistock.

Kohut, H. (1977). *The Analysis of the Self*. New York: International Universities Press.

Kolb, D. A. (1984). *Experiential Learning*. Englewood Cliffs, N.J.: Prentice Hall.

Kotlowitz, A. (1987). Changes among families prompt a vanishing sense of community. *The Wall Street Journal*. March.

Krantz, J. (1978). *Scruples*. New York: Crown Publications, Inc.

_____ (1986). *I'll Take Manhattan*. New York: Bantam Books.

Kuhn, T. S. (1972). *The Structure of Scientific Revolution,* 2nd ed. Chicago: University of Chicago Press.

_____ (1977). *Second Thoughts on Paradigma*. Urbana: The University of Illinois Press.

Lacan, J. (1966). *Ecrits*. Paris: Seuil.

Lasch, C. (1979). *The Culture of Narcissism*. New York: Warner Books.

Lévi-Strauss, C. (1949). *Les Structures Elementaries de la Parenté*. Paris: P.U.F.

Lewin, K. (1947). Frontiers in group dynamics. *Human Relations* 1:5–41.

Manfredi, S. (1979). La Linea D'ombra delle Psicoterapie. Florence: Del Riccio.

McCarthy, B. (1980). *Teaching to Learning Styles with Right Left Mode Techniques*. Barrington: Excell.

Neri, C. (1983). Le microallucinazioni. *Gruppo e Funzione Analitica* 2:21.

Newel, A. and Simon, M. A. (1972). *Human Problem Solving*. Englewood Cliffs, N.J.: Prentice Hall.

Packard, V. (1957). *The Hidden Persuaders*. New York: David McKay Co., Inc.

Prieto, L. (1966). *Messages et Signaux*. Paris: P.U.F.

Reed, L. D. (1987). Why all the world loves a soap. *Time*. March 15.

Reinemer, M. (1987). A hard look at modern bonding. *The Wall Street Journal*. May.

Richards, B. (1987). Heresy in New York. In families, singles, yuppies: who are the middle class? *The Wall Street Journal*. March.

Robbins, H. (1949). *The Dream Merchants*. Alfred A. Kropf, Inc.

Russell, B. (1983). *Los Procesos de la Filosofia*. Barcelona: Labor.

Sartre, J. P. (1960). *Critique de la Raison Dialectique*. Paris: Gallimard.

Seligman, M. E. P. (1975). *Helplessness: On Depression, Death and Development*. San Francisco: Freeman.

Sheldon, S. (1982). *Master of the Game.* New York: William Morrow & Co., Inc.

Smith, D. (1986). What would Freud think? *New York Times Magazine.* March 31.

Sperry, R. W. (1973). Lateral specialization of cerebral function in the surgically separated hemispheres. In *The Physiology of Thinking,* ed. F. J. McGuigan and R. A. Schoonover. New York: Academic Press.

Spitz, R. A. (1945). *Hospitalism. The Psychoanalytic Study of the Child.* New York: International Universities Press.

Steiner, C. (1974). *Scripts People Live.* New York: Bantam Books.

Tarski, A. (1956). *Logic, Semantics and Metamathematics.* Oxford: J.M. Woodper.

Thérive, A. (1960). L'infraliterature. Table Ronde No. 148.

Torrance, E. P. (1984). *Your Style of Learning and Thinking.* Athens, Georgia: University of Georgia Press.

Viderman, S. (1970). *La Construction de l'Espace Analytique.* Paris: Denoel.

Watzlawick, P., Weakland, J., and Fish, R. (1974). *Change: Principles of problem formulation and problem resolution.* New York: W. W. Norton.

Watzlawick, P. (1976). *How Real is Real?* New York: Random House.

Weber, B. (1987). Alone together. The unromantic generation. *The New York Times Magazine.* April 5.

Young, G. (1987). Smart hubbies mean "brighter" future for wives. *The Daily Journal.* Caracas. April.

Zajonc, R. B. (1980). Feeling and thinking: preference needs no inference. *American Psychologist.* February.

INDEX

Addiction
　defensive, resolving, 92–95
　drug, "not enough syndrome" and, 79–86
　overcoming, 113–114
　social, 8–9
　telemelodrama, 61–62
Alliance(s). *See also* Couple(s)
　command group, 170–171
　resolutive, selection of, 148–149
　therapist-patient, 128–131
Analogic cognitive style, 178–179
　couple and, 204–207
　high-level, 184–186
　low-level, 189–190
　medium-level, 187–188
Analytic setting, 119
Anomie
　defenses and, 28–28
　identification and, 26–27
Antimelodramatic alliance, 128
Antimelodramatic "otherectomy," 150
Anxiety, 5
　confronting, 106–107
　escape from, 8–9
　signal, 7
　traumatic, 7
Anxiety avoidance
　mechanisms of, 52–53
　through melodrama, 35–40. *See also* Melodrama
Artificial "morphines," 83–86
Authoritarian union, 208
Authority, interpersonal, 192–193
Avoidance. *See also* Escape
　defensive, 36, 99–100

Castration complex, 27–28, 35, 100–101
　avoiding awareness of, 52–53
Censorship, defensive avoidance and, 36
Cerebral hemispheres, 177–179
Cocaine, 83
Coding level, 181–183. *See also* Dreamers, types of
　couple and, 202–207
Cognitive style
　coding level and, 181–183
　complementarity of, couple and, 197–201
　personality and, 177–180
　types of dreamers and, 183–191
Command group, 170–171
Competence. *See also* Emotional incompetence
　gaining, 91–96
　therapeutic, 93–95

Competent lucidity, from indolent limbo to, 145, 146
Corrective "reparenting," 101
Countertransference, 138, 139
Couple(s)
  coding typology and, 204–207
  formation of
    coding levels and, 202–204
    power typology and, 207–209
  style complementarity and, 197–201
  with symmetrical styles, 202
Crisis containment, 131–133

Death instinct, life instinct and, 39–40
Defense(s)
  anomie and, 28–29
  dealing with, 163–164
Defense mechanisms, intrapsychic, 52–53, 63
Defensive addiction, resolving, 92–95
Defensive avoidance, 36
Defensive escape, 99–100
Defensive "ghetto," 8–9
Defensive monothematic inverted speech, 43–47, 54
Deficits, dealing with, 163–164
Delusions, illusions and, dreams, 5–9
Demagogic union, 208
Democratic personality, 193
  couple formation and, 207–208
Denaturalizing, 158
Depression, 5
Desire, instinct and, 39–40
Digital cognitive style, 178–180
  couple and, 204–207
  high-level, 186–187
  low-level, 190–191
  medium-level, 188–189
Displacement
  recentering, 144–147

  telemelodrama and, 62–63
Distancing, 150
Dogmatic superego, 112
Downward spiral, 84–86
Dreamers, types of, 183–191
  analogic flatlander, 187–188
  analogic highlander, 184–186
  analogic lowlander, 189–190
  couple and, 204–207
  digital flatlander, 188–189
  digital highlander, 186–187
  digital lowlander, 190–191
Drug addiction, "not enough syndrome" and, 79–86
Dyad(s). See Alliance(s); Couple(s)

Ego ideal
  ego and, 15–16
  tyranny of, 81–82
Ego psychology, 163
Emotional escapism, 6–8
Emotional incompetence
  early signs, 23–30
    identification and hypnotic state, 26–27
    paleoenvironment and, 29–30
    power envy, 27–29
  interpersonal, 24
  melodrama and. See Melodrama
  social, 24
  transformation into competence, 91–96
Emotional pain, defense against, 35–36
Endorphines, 6–7
Enemies, identification of, 115–116
Enrichment of dreams, 99–120
  challenging frame construction, 108
  direct representation of melodrama, 106
  dogmatic superego and, 112
  facing fear, 106–107

identifying friends and enemies, 115–116
making melodramatic metaconscious, 104–105
new dreams and options, 109–111
overcoming psychoaddiction, 113–114
paradigmatic psychoanalysis in, 101–102
pleasure principle vs reality principle, 111–112
psychic spaces and, 102–104
resistances to, 117–120
therapist as superego, 116–117
transunconscious, 114–115
Enthusiasm, 18–20
Envious voyeurist, 79–81
Environmental interventions, indirect, 149–150
Environmental reorganizations, 133
Escape
from anxiety, 8–9. *See also* Anxiety avoidance
defensive, 99–100
narcissistic, 52–53
therapist as accomplice, 138
Escape principle, seeking principle vs, 111–112
Escapism
emotional, 6–8. *See also* Emotional incompetence; Melodrama narcissistic, 52–53
Exhibitionism, telemelodrama and, 63
drug addiction and, 83–86
Exorphines, 6
Experimental insight, 94

"Facts," establishment of, 141–143
Family life, in Freud's time, 24–26
Family myth, 160
Fear, facing, 106–107
"Flatlander," 183
analogic, 187–188

couple and, 205–206
digital, 188–189
Frame analysis, "from above," 157–159
Frame construction, challenging, 108
Freud, Sigmund, 14
environment of, family life in, 24–26
Friends, identification of, 115–116

Happiness
health and, upward spiral to, 91–92
production of 13–14
search for, flight from unhappiness vs, 7–8
sense of, 18–20
triangle of, 13–14, 15
Health
happiness and, upward spiral to, 91–92
mental, definition, 13
Helplessness, learned, 35
High-level personality ("highlander"), 183
analogic, 184–186
couple and, 204–205
digital, 186–187
Hypnotic state, identification and 26–27
Hysteria, 25

Ideal of the ego
ego and, 15–16
tyranny of, 81–82
Identification. *See also* Teleidentification
hypnotic state and, 26–27
projective, 45–47
Illusions, delusions and, dreams vs, 5–9
Impotency complex, 100–101

Incompetence
  emotional. *See* Emotional incompetence
  politico-economic, 191–192
In-depth interpretation, 119
Indolent limbo
  competent lucidity vs, 145, 146
  mastered reality vs, 171–173
Insight, experiential, 94
Insolvent personality, 191–192
Instinct, desire and, 39–40
"Intelligentizing" action, 209
Interpersonal authority, 192–193
Interpersonal incompetence, 24
Interpersonal melodrama, 38–39
Interpretation, in-depth, 119
Intrapsychic defense mechanisms, 52–53, 63
Inverted speech, monothematic, defensive, 43–47, 54

Latent content, 47
Learned helplessness, 35
Left brain personality, 178–179. *See also* Cognitive style
Life instinct, death instinct and, 39–40
Limbo
  lucidity vs, 145, 146
  reality vs, 171–173
Low-level personality ("lowlander"), 183
  analogic, 189–190
  couple and, 206–207
  digital, 190–191
Lucidity, from limbo to, 145, 146

Manifest melodrama, 124–128
Masochism
  mirrorism and, 56
  sadism and, in melodrama, 43–47. *See also* Melodrama
Masochistic agents, 193

Masochistic patients, 194
Mastered reality, from indolent limbo to, 171–173
Meaningful project, implementation of, 157–173
  command group, 170–171
  dealing with defenses and deficits, 163–164
  frame analysis "from above," 157–159
  from indolent limbo to mastered reality, 171–173
  motivational switch, 159–160
  socially shared pet theories, 160–161
  therapeutic triangularization, 162–163
  using strengths, 169
  value qualification challenge, 161–162
  working out, 164–169
Medium-level personality ("flatlander"), 183
  analogic, 187–188
  couple and, 205–206
  digital, 188–189
Melodrama. *See also* Telemelodrama
  anxiety avoidance through, 35–40
  definition, 37
  direct representation of, 106
  masking, 124–128
  metaconscious and, 104–105
  personal vs interpersonal, 37–39
  pleasure principle and, 111
  protagonists, 43–47
  romanticism vs, 17–18
  sadomasochistic and narcissistic monologue in, 51–57
  stepping out of, 137–151
    establishing "facts," 141–143
    indirect environmental interventions, 149–150
    recentering on what is displaced, 144–147

Index

therapeutic goal, 150–151
transforming meloenvironment, 147–149
working through transference, 138–141
Melodramatic frame, analysis of, "from above," 157–159
Melodream, 45–47
Meloenvironment, 45
transformation of, 147–149
Mental Health
definition, 13
happiness and, upward spiral to, 91–92
Mental illness, 23–24. *See also* Emotional incompetence
paleoenvironment and, 30
Metaconscious, 55
development of, 142
melodrama in, 104–105
psychic spaces and, 103–104
resistances to, 117–120
therapist's, 95–96
Meta-incompetence, 29–30
"Metasolving" problems, 95–96
Mirrorist, narcissist and, 55–57
Monologue, sadomasochistic and narcissistic, 51–57
Monothematic inverted speech, defensive, 43–47, 54
"Morphines," 6–7
artificial, 83–86
Motivational switch, 92, 159–160

Narcissism, 51–52. *See also* Melodrama
Narcissist, mirrorist and, 55–57
Narcissistic escape mechanisms, 52–53
Narcissistic monologue, 51–57
Neoenvironment, 29
command group in, 170–171
Neomind, 29
Neoparadigm, 158

New dreams, 109–111
"Not enough syndrome," drug addiction and, 79–86

Pain, defense against, 35–36
Paleoenvironment, 29–30
limitations, perception of, 35
Paradigmatic psychoanalysis, 111–112
personal paradigms and, 101–102
Paradoxical protest, 73–75
Parenting
corrective, 101
phallic, 27–28, 29
uterine, 29
Pathogenic frame, therapeutic frame vs, 113
Pathogenic options, 84–86
Pentadimensional topology, 54–55
Personality
coding level and, 182–183
cognitive style and, 177–180
couples and. *See* Couple(s)
democratic vs totalitarian, 192–193
power typology and, 193–194
solvent vs insolvent, 191–192
types of dreamers, 183–191. *See also* Dreamers, types of
Personal paradigms, paradigmatic psychoanalysis and, 101–102
Pet theories, socially shared, 160–161
Phallic parenting, 27–28, 29
Pleasure principle, reality principle and, 111–112
Politico-economic power, 191–192
Power envy, 27–29
Power typology, 193–194
couple formation and, 207–209
Preconscious frame, challenging, 108
Problem solving
"metasolving," 95–96
specific and general, 128–131

Projective identification, 45–47
  reintrojection of projected, 144
Protest, paradoxical, 73–75
Pseudodream, melodramatic, 45–47
Psychic spaces
  therapeutic goals and, 102–104
Psychoaddiction, 9
  overcoming, 113–114
Psychoanalysis. *See also*
    Therapeutic *entries;* Therapy
  paradigmatic, 101–102, 111–112
  traditional approaches to, 163
Psychodialysis, 9
Psychotherapy, 91. *See also* Therapeutic *entries;* Therapy

Realism, romanticism and, 19–20
Reality, mastered, from indolent limbo to, 171–173
Reality principle, pleasure principle and, 111–112
Reframing of dreams, 99–120
  challenging frame construction, 108
  direct representation of melodrama, 106
  dogmatic superego and, 112
  facing fear, 106–107
  identifying friends and enemies, 115–116
  making melodramatic metaconscious, 104–105
  new dreams and options, 109–111
  overcoming psychoaddiction, 113–114
  paradigmatic psychoanalysis in, 101–102
  pleasure principle vs reality principle, 111–112
  psychic spaces and, 102–104
  resistances to, 117–120
  therapist as superego, 116–117
  transunconscious enrichment, 114–115

"Reparenting," corrective, 101
Repetition compulsion, 45–47
Repressed story, uncovering, 123–133
  crisis containment, 131–133
  masking melodrama and, 124–128
  problem solving in, 128–131
  transference in therapy and, 123–124
Resistances
  major and minor, 117–120
  to value qualification challenges, 161–162
Resolutive allies, selection of, 148–149
Right brain personality, 177–179.
  See also Cognitive style
Romanticism
  melodrama vs, 17–18
  realism and, 19–20, 111–112

Sadism
  masochism and, in melodrama, 43–47. *See also* Melodrama
  narcissism and, 56
Sadistic agents, 193
Sadistic insufficients, 193
Sadistic patients, 193
Sadomasochistic complicity, 44–45
Sadomasochistic monologue, 51–57
Sclerophrenia, 92, 93
Seeking principle, escape principle vs, 111–112
Self, symbolic togetherness with, 16–17
Self-preservation instinct, 39
Self-realization, 100
Sensible method, from dogmatic superego to, 112
Sentimentalism, addiction to. *See* Melodrama
Sexual instinct, 39
Shared transcendence, 13

Index

Signal anxiety, 7
Soap operas. *See* Telemelodrama
Social addiction, 8–9
Social incompetence, 24
Socially shared pet theories, 160–161
Solvent personality, 191–192
Speech, inverted, defensive monothematic, 43–47, 54
Strengths, use of, 169
Style complementarity, couple and, 197–201
Success, definition, 13
Superego
  dogmatic, 112
  of superego, therapist as, 116–117
Survival
  defensive escape and, 99–100
  self-realization and, 100
Symbolic elaboration, degrees of, 181–183
Symbolic togetherness, 15–17

Teleaddiction, 61–62
Teledisplacement, 62–63, 64
Teleidentification, 26–27, 64–65
Telemelodrama, 37–39, 61–66. *See also* Melodrama
  I'll Take Manhattan as prototype, 69–75
  pushers and users, 69–75
"Teletogetherness," 16–17
Televoyeurism, 63–64
Therapeutic contract, 139
Therapeutic frame, pathogenic frame vs, 113
Therapeutic goal(s), 130–131
  psychic spaces and, 102–104
  as strategic decision, 150–151
Therapeutic option, 173
Therapeutic process, romanticism and realism in, 20

Therapeutic restructuring, 150
Therapeutic strategy, 197–216
  coding levels and couple formation, 202–204
  coding typology and couple, 204–207
  couples with symmetrical styles and, 202
  power typology and couple formation, 207–209
  style complementarity and couple, 197–201
  typologies and, 209–216
Therapeutic triangularizing, 162–163
Therapist
  as accomplice to escape, 138
  as superego, 116–117
Therapy. *See also specific aspect*
  approach to, 163
  corrective "reparenting" in, 101
  indirect environmental interventions in, 149–150
  problem solving in, 128–131
  resistances to, 117–120
  tasks of, 100
  transference in, 123–124
Togetherness
  romanticism vs melodrama and, 17–18
  symbolic, 15–17
Topological spaces, redimensioning, 54–55, 103
Totalitarian personality, 193
  couple formation and, 208–209
Transcendence, 14–16
  romanticism vs melodrama and, 17–18
  sense of happiness and, 18–20
  shared, 13
  symbolic togetherness and, 15–17
  well-being and, 14
Transference
  in therapy, 123–124
  working through, 138–141

Transunconscious enrichment, 114–115
Transunconscious extraframe space, 109–111
Traumatic anxiety, 7
Treatment. *See* Therapeutic *entries;* Therapy; *specific aspect*
Triangle of happiness, 13–14, 15
Triangularization, therapeutic, 162–163
Typologies. *See also* Coding level; Cognitive style; Personality; Power typology
    therapeutic implications of, 209–216

Unconscious
  making metaconscious, resistances to, 117–120
  in pentadimensional topology, 55
  psychoanalysis of, 163
Unhappiness, flight from, 7–8
Untold story, 124
Upward spiral, 91–92
Uterine parenting, 29

Value qualifications, challenging, 161–162
Voyeurism
  envious, 79–81
  telemelodrama and, 63–64

Well-being, transcendence and, 14
Working out, after working through, 164–169
Working through, transference, 138–141